THE PROPHECIES OF
NOSTRADAMUS

THE PROPHECIES OF
NOSTRADAMUS

**GEDDES &
GROSSET**

Published 2006 by Geddes & Grosset
David Dale House
New Lanark
ML11 9DJ

Copyright © 2006 Geddes & Grosset

All rights reserved. No part of this publication may be reproduced, stored in a retrieval system, or transmitted, in any form or by any means, electronic, mechanical, photocopying, recording or otherwise without the prior permission of the copyright holder

ISBN 10 1 84205 523 2
ISBN 13 978 1 84205 523 6

Printed and bound in Poland

Contents

Introduction 7

The Prophecies 11

Introduction

Michel de Nostredame was an intriguing character who was born on 14 December 1503 in Provence. He was Jewish by descent, and his father, Jacques, was the son of Pierre de Nostredame, a grain dealer, and his wife, Blanche. Nostradamus' father moved from the Avignon district to St Rémy in Provence towards the end of the fifteenth century, where he gave up the family business. Nostradamus was one of five brothers, about whom little is known, but his early childhood in the Jewish faith was influenced by his grandfather Jean, who taught him much, including mathematics, Greek, Hebrew, some Latin and astrology. When he was nine, the family were converted to Catholicism from Judaism, but the Jewish aspect of the boy's life proves significant later in deciphering his prophecies.

It was quickly noticed that Nostradamus was a more than able pupil—indeed, he was brilliant. His grandfather Jean died but when Nostradamus returned to his parents' home, his education was continued by his paternal grandfather, Pierre. While still a teenager he was sent to study at Avignon, where he often caused a stir with his outspoken beliefs, one of which was that the Earth was round and that it moved around the Sun—a dangerously extreme view for that age. However, in 1522 he went to the University of Montpelier to study medicine at the famous institution there. He gained his degree after just three years and upon receiving his licence to practice medicine, he went around the country to help the numerous victims of the plague.

Nostradamus seemed unafraid to try new and different approaches, and in fighting the plague he created his own methods of treatment and new, unorthodox medicines. In fact he met with considerable success and became well known for this and for his kind and sympathetic treatment of the victims. He travelled quite widely, to Toulouse, Bordeaux and elsewhere, and his travels were interspersed with periods of study. Also at this time he developed an interest in the occult, alchemy and magic, topics he pursued in the library at Avignon. In 1529 he returned to Montpelier to complete his doctorate, and although his fame had gone before him, often to his detriment, his ability could not be denied, and he obtained his doctoral degree.

He again commenced his travels, just one year after joining the faculty at Montpelier (a position he found very confining), and again visited Toulouse. While there he was invited to visit the philosopher, Scaliger, at Agen. He stayed there and married a young woman from a wealthy family with whom he raised two children. All seemed to be going well for Nostradamus until the plague struck the town and his family fell victim to its ravages. His previous good fortunes then deserted him rapidly, and in addition to his personal loss, he argued with Scaliger and, the final straw, he was accused of heresy and ordered to appear before the Inquisitors at Toulouse. Not surprisingly, he did not find this prospect particularly inviting and so he decided, once again, to travel, avoiding the Church authorities for the next six years. He finally settled in a southern town, Salon, having first gone to Marseilles to help victims of flood and plague.

In 1550, Nostradamus published his first almanac, which contained predictions for the coming year. This proved very successful, and so Nostradamus made it an annual event. Just a few years later, he had the idea of writing the Centuries that would make up the prophecies. He turned the top room of his house in Salon into a study, working at night with his books on the occult. The predictions dealt with events from his time to the end of the world, which was put at the year 3797. Nostradamus' Centuries have no connotation of time—it is merely that his quatrains (four-lined verse) were grouped in hundreds. By 1555, about a year after starting, Nostradamus had completed the first part of his task, which was to write ten Centuries, that is one thousand quatrains. In fact Century 7 was not finished, and there is evidence that he wrote some quatrains for Centuries 11 and 12.

Introduction

The quatrains are written in a peculiar fashion and are deliberately obscure. This was to avoid him being labelled as a magician. He used a very mixed vocabulary comprising French, Latin and Provençal with some Greek and Italian. The Prophecies became very popular at the royal court, one of the few places where they could be read, since it was necessary to have money and an education to purchase and read such a volume. Royalty also became intrigued—Catherine de' Medici sent for Nostradamus and he also had a brief audience with Henri III.

The complete *Prophecies of Nostradamus* was not actually published until 1568, two years after his death. He was buried in one of the walls of a church at Salon although his remains were unearthed during the French Revolution. He was, however, interred again in another Salon church, the Church of St Laurent. His grave and portrait can be seen there to this day.

The *Prophecies of Nostradamus* has generated a great deal of interest since it was first published and there is much confusion about the early editions of the book. There were numerous fake versions, an undertaking rendered more likely by the absence of a date on some of the oldest volumes.

It is not surprising that the Prophecies have been used for propaganda purposes over the centuries. Strong links have been drawn with the French Revolution and the exploits of Napoleon, but word of Nostradamus was not limited to France. He became known all over Europe within twenty to thirty years. In more recent times, Adolf Hitler became interested in the quatrains and actually dropped printed selections on France in an attempt to influence the behaviour of the French people.

Inevitably, some regard Nostradamus as a fraud, others as a prophet. He thought that he had some powers, but of course these were not infallible. It may be prophecy or mere guesswork aided by generally vague predictions and a willing interpreter. However, many feel that although much can be written off as coincidental or as being applicable to numerous diverse events, there are some predictions that are difficult to ignore—the details are just too accurate. Or are they?

This book contains a fascinating selection of the Prophecies of Nostradamus, arranged chronologically according to the events they predict.

The Prophecies

1202

Le plus grand voile hors du port de Zara,
Prés de Bisance fera son entreprise;
D'ennemy perte & l'amy ne fera,
Le tiers à deux fera grand pille & prise.

The greatest sail out of the port of Zara, near Byzantium shall he carry out his enterprise. There shall not be loss of enemies and friends, the third will turn on the two and make great pillage and capture.

In this quatrain Nostradamus may have been describing events that took place three hundred years earlier during the Fourth Crusade. The Venetians (Zara) agreed to join the Crusade provided that a large amount of money was paid to them and that they would be entitled to half the spoils. The Crusaders were not able to find the necessary fee and instead captured Zara and were excommunicated by the Pope. They went on to capture and pillage Byzantium (Istanbul) and to found Romania.

[*Century 8, quatrain 83*]

1512

Champ Perusin, ô l'enorme deffaite
Et le conflict tout aupres de Rauenne;
Passage sacre lors qu'on fera la feste,
Vainqueur vaincu cheval manger l'avenne.

Perugian battlefield, O what an enormous defeat and the conflict very close to Ravenna. A sacred passage when they shall celebrate the feast, the victorious vanquished, the horse to eat up his feed.

Nostradamus may have been referring to an event that took place in his early childhood, the Battle at Ravenna in 1512. Ravenna and Perugia belonged to the papacy and fell to forces led by Gaston de Foix.

[*Century 8, quatrain 72*]

1517

L'arc du thresor par Achilles deceu,
Aux procrees sceu la quadrangulaire;
Au faict Royal le comment sera sceu,
Corps veu pendu au veu du populaire.

The arch of the treasurer by Achilles deceived, to the procreators shall make known the quadrangle. In the royal deed the comment shall be known, the corpse shall be seen hung in the sight of the populace.

Achille de Harlay, who was President of the Parliament of Paris, exposed the fraudulent practices of Marshal d'Ancre, the Treasurer of France. The marshal was a favourite of Marie de' Medici, who was queen regent, but even this patronage failed to save him. He was accused and convicted of the misappropriation of funds and was killed, on the orders of Louis XIII, in a quadrangle of the Louvre Palace. His body was later hung up to the public gaze.

[*Century 7, quatrain 1*]

1543–1650

Des plus lettrez dessus les faits celestes,
Seront par princes ignorans reprouuez;
Punis d'edit, chassez comme celestes,
Et mis à mort là où seront trouuez.

Some of the most learned in the celestial arts will be reproved by ignorant princes; punished by an edict, chased away as scoundrels and put to death wherever they shall be found.

The Inquisition was a powerful and feared organization in Nostradamus' time, and this quatrain refers to its activities. Various learned men were constrained by the Inquisition, especially Galileo, who reaffirmed (in 1632) the earlier theory of Copernicus (1543) that the heavenly bodies were in orbit around the sun. Galileo was forced to recant publicly in 1633 because of the fearful consequences of opposing the Inquisition. René Descartes, the French philosopher and mathematician, in his writings, *Discours de la Méthode*, in 1637, argued for the advancement of knowledge based on scientific principles. He rejected the concept that the Church, or any other body, was the final arbiter of truth and believed that the intellect of each individual was of vital importance in the pursuance of knowledge and faith.

This was anathema to the ruling powers of the Church and Inquisition, monarch and state, and when Descartes, who was always a devout Catholic, died, Louis XIV made sure that he did not have a Christian burial. The activities of the Inquisition had the effect of diverting the quest for scientific knowledge away from the Catholic countries to the Protestant lands of Northern Europe, where scientists and philosophers did not face torture and persecution. In 1538, Nostradamus himself was summoned to appear before the Inquisition at Toulouse, accused of heresy. He was forced to make himself scarce and assumed a low profile, travelling around France and staying away from Church authorities for a period of six years.

[*Century 4, quatrain 18*]

1552–1570

Le grand Pilot sera par Roy mandé
Laisser la classe, pour plus haut lieu attaindre;
Sept ans après sera contrebandé,
Barbare armée viendra Venise craindre.

The great pilot shall be sent for by royal mandate to leave the fleet to attain a higher position. Seven years after he shall be smuggling, a barbarian army shall make Venice come to fear.

One person to whom this quatrain may apply is Gaspard de Coligny, who was appointed Admiral of the French Navy by Henri II in 1552 ('the great pilot'). When the king was accidentally killed in 1559, de Coligny relinquished the post and became involved with the Calvinist cause and the conflict between the Huguenots (French Protestants) and Catholics. At that time, Venice and the Venetians were being attacked by the 'barbarian army' of Sultan Selim II and were defeated in Cyprus in 1570.

[*Century 6, quatrain 75*]

1555

L'impotent prince fasché, plaines & querelles,
De raps & pillés par coqs & par lybiques,
Grand est par terre, par mer infinies voilles,
Seule Italie sera chassant Celtiques.

The powerless prince angry, complaints and quarrels, of rapes and pillage carried out by the cocks and by the libiques. It is great by land, by sea infinite sails; Italy alone shall be driving out the Celts.

The 'cocks' represent the French and the 'libiques' are Algerian troops who joined forces with them in the battles for Elba and its surrounding kingdoms. The 'powerless prince' is probably Cosimo de' Medici, Duke of Florence, who was in charge of the defending forces against the French. Nostradamus was mistaken in that Italy did not drive out the French on this occasion.

[Century 4, quatrain 4]

Fustes & galees autour de sept navires,
Sera librée une mortelle guerre;
Chef de Madric recevra coup de vires,
Deux eschapées, & cinq menées à terre.

Frigates and galleys around about seven ships, a mortal war shall be liberated. The leader from Madrid shall receive a wound from arrows, two shall escape and five carried to land.

This verse may describe an event in the winter of 1555. A fleet of Spanish vessels in the English Channel were attacked by pirates from Dieppe. The ship commanded by the Spanish Admiral was boarded and seized, and he was wounded. Four other Spanish ships were captured and all were taken back to Dieppe.

[*Century 7, quatrain 26*]

1555–1557

Le grand Duc d'Albe se viendra rebeller,
À ses grands pères fera le tradiment;
Le grand de Guise le viendra debeller,
Captif mené & dressé monument.

The great Duke of Alba shall come to rebel, to his grandfathers he shall make the treachery. The great one of Guise shall come to vanquish him, led captive and a monument erected.

This quatrain evidently refers to the Duke of Alba and the Duke de Guise, but it is not accurate historically. The Duke de Guise did not capture the Duke of Alba but the latter did join the French side in war against the Pope and the Vatican.

[*Century 7, quatrain 29*]

1557

La gent Gauloise & nation étrange,
Outre les monts morts, prins & profligez;
Au moys contraire & proche de vendange
Par les Seigneurs en accord redigez.

The French people and a foreign nation across the mountains shall be killed and captured. In a month contrary to the interests and near the time of the grape vintage, by the lords in agreement drawn up.

This may refer to the terms for peace agreed between the Pope and Spanish forces in September 1557 ('vendage' in the original French may mean either the general harvest or the grape gathering itself, which took place in September). The concerns of the Duke of Guise, whose troops were fighting for the Pope, were totally disregarded on this occasion.

[*Century 3, quatrain 38*]

1557

> *La grand cité d'assaut pront & repentin,*
> *Surprins de nuict, gardes interrompus;*
> *Les excubies & veilles saint Quintin,*
> *Trucidez gardes & les portails rompus.*

The great city by a sudden assault taken, surprised by night, the guards interrupted; the watch and guard of St Quentin slain and the gates broken down.

The town of St Quentin was captured in 1557, not by a sudden attack but as a result of a siege that lasted for eighteen days. The final attack and overrunning of the town perhaps came as a surprise, which seems to be indicated here.

[Century 4, quatrain 8]

> *Grand cité à soldats abandonnée,*
> *Onc ny eut mortel tumult si proche,*
> *O qu'elle hideuse calamité s'approche,*
> *Fors une offense n'y sera pardonnée.*

The great city to the soldiers shall be abandoned, there never was a mortal tumult so near. Oh! What a hideous calamity approaches, except for one offence nothing shall be pardoned.

This is a very general description of the fall of a great city during battle and could apply to almost any period of warfare throughout the centuries. However, many commentators believe that Nostradamus was thinking of the fall of St Quentin in 1557, although many other examples right up to the present day are equally applicable. It is certain that the inhabitants suffered almost total slaughter, with the possible exception of those in league with the aggressors.

[Century 6, quatrain 96]

1557

> *Prés de Quintin dans la forest Bourlis,*
> *Dans l'Abbaye seront Flamens tranchés;*
> *Les deux puisnais de coups my estourdis,*
> *Suitte oppressée & garde tous hachés.*

Near St Quentin in the forest of Bourlis, in the Abbey shall the Flemish be slashed. The two youngest half-stunned by blows, the followers oppressed and the guard cut to pieces.

On the eve of the Battle of St Quentin, which occurred in August 1557, the Spanish forces took control of the Abbey of Vermandois and, presumably, two young brothers fell victim in the manner described.

[*Century 9, quatrain 40*]

> *Gardon à Nemans eaux si hault desborderont,*
> *Qu'on cuidera Deucalion renaistre,*
> *Dans le colosse la plus part fuyront,*
> *Vesta sepulchre feu estaint apparoistre.*

Gardon to Nîmes, so high will it flood that they think Deucalion has been born again. In the colossus the larger part will flee, and Vesta's fire appears in the sepulchre, extinguished.

In 1557, there was a great flood of the River Gardon. Nostradamus predicts this event to be similar to the great flood that Zeus inflicted upon the world. At that time, the only survivors were Deucalion and his wife. The flood was accompanied by a great storm, and a number of antiquities were exposed after the waters subsided. It has to be said that despite the specific reference to the River Gardon, much of the latter part of the quatrain is obscure.

[*Century 10, quatrain 6*]

1558

Lors que celuy qu'à nul ne donne lieu,
Abandonner voudra lieu prins non prins;
Feu, nef, par saignes, bitument à Charlieu,
Seront Quintin, Balez reprins.

When he that will give place to none shall abandon a place taken and not taken; fire, ship, by the swamps, bitumen at Charlieu, then St Quintin and Calais shall be retaken.

This quatrain appears to refer to naval warfare in the middle of the sixteenth century. Calais was recaptured for the French by the Duke de Guise in 1558 and St Quentin was returned by negotiation in 1559.

[*Century 9, quatrain 29*]

1558–1560

Premier fils vefue mal'heureux mariage,
Sans nuls enfans deux Isles en discord,
Avant dixhuit incompetant aage,
De l'autre prés plus bas sera l'accord.

The first son, a widow, an unhappy marriage with no children, two islands in discord. Before eighteen, an incompetent age, of the other even lower will be the agreement.

The relationship between Francis II and Mary Stuart (Queen of Scots) is described quite accurately in this quatrain. Francis was the eldest son of Catherine de' Medici and in 1558 he married Mary Stuart. The marriage was blighted, there were no children, and in 1560 Francis died. The discord probably refers to that between England and Scotland, which was caused by Mary's return to Scotland.

[*Century 10, quatrain 39*]

> *Les mal'heureuses nopces celebreront*
> *En grande joye mais la fin mal'heureuse;*
> *Mary & mère nore desdaigneront,*
> *Le Phybe mort, & nore plus piteuse.*

The ill-fated nuptials with great joy will be celebrated, but the end is unhappy. Mary and the mother-in-law will disdain each other, the Phybe is dead and the daughter-in-law much to be pitied.

This quatrain applies to the short, unhappy marriage of Mary Queen of Scots and Francis II, and it is well established that Mary and her mother-in-law had a mutual dislike of each other.

[*Century 10, quatrain 55*]

1558–1562

> *L'election faicte dans Francfort,*
> *N'aura nul lieu, Milan s'opposera;*
> *Le sien plus proche semblera si grand fort,*
> *Qu'outre le Rhinés mareschs chassera.*

The election made in Frankfurt shall be null and void, Milan will oppose it. His own close one shall seem so very strong that he will chase him out beyond the Rhine marshes.

The coronation of Ferdinand I as Holy Roman Emperor took place in Milan in 1559. It occurred because his brother, Charles V, had abdicated in 1556, leaving his son, Philip II, to inherit the most valuable parts of his kingdom, although the title of

'Emperor' was given to Ferdinand. Philip II considered that he had the rightful claim to Milan, and this quatrain indeed seems to suggest that Ferdinand's election was 'null and void'. Philip tried unsuccessfully to drive Ferdinand out of Milan and continued to plot against him until 1562.

[*Century 6, quatrain 87*]

1558–1603

Là dechassée au regne tournera,
Ses ennemis trouvez des conjurez;
Plus que jamais son temps triomphera,
Trois & septante à mort trop asseurez.

She who was rejected shall return to reign, her enemies shall be found to be conspirators. More than ever shall her time be triumphant, three and seventy at death very sure.

These lines appear to describe aptly the life and reign of Queen Elizabeth I of England, 'Good Queen Bess', a time that is still regarded as a golden age. Elizabeth experienced rejection during her childhood—by her father, Henry VIII, who was interested only in sons, and by the execution of her mother, Anne Boleyn, in 1536, which left her very much alone and friendless. In childhood and young adulthood she lived not only with rejection but also with plots and intrigues that threatened her life. Even when she ascended the throne as queen, the third and last of Henry's children to do so, she was beset by enemies and conspiracies, as described in the quatrain. Much of the intrigue concerned her 'cousin', Mary Stuart, Queen of Scots, who in fact had a legitimate claim to England's throne. History bears out the fact that Elizabeth was a shrewd and successful monarch who overcame all opposition and inspired the love of her people. England became a major power in world affairs during her reign and produced explorers, writers, artists and scientists. She died in 1603 at the age of seventy so Nostradamus was slightly mistaken here.

[*Century 6, quatrain 74*]

> *Jour que sera par Royne saluée,*
> *Le jour après le salut, la priere;*
> *Le comte fait raison & valbuée,*
> *Par avant humble oncques ne fut si fiere.*

The day that she will be saluted as queen, the day after the blessing the prayer; the account is right and paid, she that was humble before never was so proud.

Another quatrain that aptly describes Elizabeth I of England who rose from an uncertain position in childhood to become a monarch of great renown.

[*Century 10, quatrain 19*]

1559

> *La paix s'approche d'un costé & la querre*
> *Oncques ne fut la poursuite si grande,*
> *Plaindre homme, femme, sang innocent par terre,*
> *Et ce sera de France à toute bande.*

Peace approaches from one side, and the war, there never was so great a pursuit. Feel sorry for man, woman, innocent blood on the land and it will be to all sides of France.

There is an apparent juxtaposition of peace and war here, which could be the cessation of hostilities between France and Spain and the subsequent French Wars of Religion that divided the country. By the middle of the sixteenth century, the Huguenots (French Protestants) were rapidly growing in number. In addition, the Catholics were divided into extremists who wanted heresy stamped out, and those of a more tolerant nature who were initially led by Catherine de' Medici. Fighting broke out in 1562, and it was only ended by Henri of Navarre when he turned Catholic and reached an agreement with his former Protestant supporters in the Edict of Nantes.

[*Century 9, quatrain 52*]

1559–1589

La dame seule au regne demeurée,
L'unique estaint premier au lict d'honneur,
Sept ans sera de douleur explorée,
Plus longue vie au regne par grand heur.

The lady shall be left to reign alone, the unique one extinguished, first in the bed of honour. For seven years she will be expressing her grief, then a long life for the great hour of her kingdom.

This is a contemporary quatrain describing events that occurred during Nostradamus' own lifetime. Henri II, King of France and husband of Catherine de' Medici, was killed in 1559, and this verse was written immediately after his death. Nostradamus may have 'played to the audience' here, for he knew that Catherine was a powerful patron and one who relied greatly on his predictions so he would also have known that she would do her best to 'live up' to her role in the prophecy. Hence Catherine did indeed mourn for her husband for seven years until 1566. No doubt she did her best to exercise her power with wisdom and restraint during the period that she was regent, but whether this was 'a great hour' for France is open to debate. Nostradamus could not have known that she would survive to a grand old age, dying at the age of nearly seventy in 1589.

[*Century 6, quatrain 63*]

> *Par lors qu'un Roy sera contre les siens,*
> *Natif de Bloys subjuguera Ligures;*
> *Mammel, Cordube & les Dalmatiens,*
> *Des sept puis l'ombre à Roy estrennes & lemures.*

Where a king will be against his own, a native of Blois will subdue the League. Mammel, Cordoba and the Dalmations, shadow of the seven, a royal present and ghost.

This is rather vague, but a few of the features are taken by some authorities to refer to Henri III, who was a descendant of the court of Blois and who subdued the Catholic League (see references to this elsewhere). The 'shadow of the seven' is taken to refer to the seven children of Catherine de' Medici, but the place names seem of little consequence or relevance, particularly Mammel, which cannot be identified with any certainty.

[*Century 10, quatrain 44*]

> *En l'an qu'un œil en France regnera,*
> *La court sera en un bien fascheux trouble;*
> *Le grand de Bloys son amy tuera,*
> *Le regne mis en mal & doute double.*

In the year that one eye shall reign in France, the court will be in one very great trouble. The great man of Blois shall kill his friend, the kingdom shall be in an evil way and double doubt.

This well-known quatrain was recognized by people in sixteenth century France to refer to King Henri II, who was fatally wounded in a friendly joust. Accidentally pierced in the eye, he died ten days later from his injury, having first forgiven his friend and assailant, Gabriel de Lorges, Count of Montgomery. The second part of the verse describes his son and third heir, Henri III, who was responsible for the murder of the Duke of Guise and his brother, Louis de Guise, Cardinal of Lorraine, at

Blois. There was continual conflict, both before and after this event, between the Catholic League and the supporters of the king, which is the 'double doubt' referred to in the quatrain. (*See also* Century 3, quatrain 30, page 29, and quatrain 51, pages 47–48.)

[*Century 3, quatrain 55*]

1560

Dedans Lyon vingt & cinq d'une halaine,
Cinq citoyens Germains, Bressans, Latins,
Par dessous noble conduiront longue traine,
Et descouvers par abbois de mastins.

In Lyons, twenty and five of the same breath, five citizens, Germans, Bressans, Latins, under a noble one they will conduct a long train and are discovered by the barking of mastiffs.

This refers to a conspiracy in 1560 to hand over the city of Lyons to the Huguenots. Five of the conspirators were natives of the city while the others included German Protestants. Many suspected that the plot had been fostered by the Prince de Conde but the plot was foiled before it could be brought to fruition, the conspirators being discovered by the military guards.

[*Century 10, quatrain 59*]

1560–1571

Cela du reste de sang non espandu,
Venise quiert secours estre donné,
Apres avoir bien long temps attendu,
Cite livree au premier cornet sonné.

The rest of the blood shall not be spilt, Venice shall seek for succour to be given. After having waited for a very long time, the city is given up at the first sound of the trumpet.

This quatrain is usually attributed to the prolonged besieging of Cyprus by Turkish forces. The Venetians hoped for aid from Christian forces, but none was given. Famagusta, the capital city of Cyprus, was subjected to a long siege but was finally forced to capitulate in 1571.

[*Century 4, quatrain 1*]

1562–1569

Le grand Baillif d'Orleans mis à mort,
Sera par un de sang vindicatif;
De mort merite ne mourra ne par fort,
Des pieds & mains mal le faisoit captif.

The great Bailiff of Orléans shall be put to death by one of vindictive blood. He shall not die a deserved death nor by fate; badly by feet and hands made captive.

In Nostradamus' time, the Bailiff of Orléans was an inherited position held by successive members of the Greslot family. In 1569, Jerôme Greslot was executed for an earlier alleged act of treachery committed in 1562. He had compromised the city's defences by opening its gates. The last line may be an obscure reference to the length of time between the offence and the sentence, and the verse as a whole indicates that the bailiff did not deserve his fate.

[*Century 3, quatrain 66*]

1564–1574

Celuy qu'en luitte & fer au fait bellique,
Aura porté plus grand que luy le pris;
De nuit au lit six luy feront la pique,
Nud sans harnois subit sera surprins.

He who in struggling and with a weapon in a warlike deed, will have carried off the prize from one greater than he, at night to his bed six will bring pikes. Naked without his armour he will suddenly be surprised.

These lines refer to the Gabriel de Lorges, Count of Montgomery, who accidentally killed his friend and sovereign, Henri II, in a jousting match. The king forgave Montgomery before he died, but Catherine de' Medici wished to see him pay for the deed with his life. The count fled to England and joined the Protestant cause. Ten years later, he returned to France to lead the rebellious Protestant forces. At first he enjoyed a number of successes, including the capture of La Rochelle, but was eventually defeated and forced to surrender by Marshal de Mantignon at Domfront. His surrender should have ensured his safety, but Catherine de' Medici had a long memory and sent six men of the royal guard to arrest him. This occurred on the night of 27 May 1574, and Montgomery was taken from his room to the Conciergerie and later executed.

[*Century 3, quatrain 30*]

1565

De l'Orient viendra le cœur Punique,
Facher Hadrie & les hoirs Romulides,
Accompagné de la classe Libique
Trembler Mellites, & proches Isles vuides.

1567

From the Orient will come the African heart to trouble Hadrie (or Venice) and the heirs of Romulus. Accompanied by the Libyan tribe, Malta and the neighbouring islands shall be deserted.

The latter half of this quatrain in all probability refers to the siege of Malta in 1565, but this is dependent upon 'tribe' being interpreted as 'fleet' (the original French is 'classe'). In this event the 'Libyan' fleet is the Turkish fleet in the Mediterranean. The first part of the quatrain either refers to Henri IV (Hadrie), with the trouble from the Orient being the Duke of Parma, or, if one again takes Hadrie as Adrie and its translation, Venice, the meaning changes dramatically. This could then refer to the part played by Emperor Haile Selassie of Ethiopia. In 1936, he was driven from his country by the Italians. In the Second World War, he reconquered Ethiopia and aided the Allies in defeating the fascists in Italy, who called themselves the 'heirs of Romulus'. (*See also* Century 1, quatrain 8, page 49.)

[*Century 1, quatrain 9*]

1567

Lettres trouvées de la Royne les coffres,
Point de subscrit sans aucun nom d'autheur,
Par la police seront cachez les offres,
Qu'on ne sçaura qui sera l'amateur.

Letters are found in the coffers of the Queen. There is neither the signature nor the name of the author. By the trick the offers shall be concealed, so that they do not know who the lover is.

The documents referred to are the 'casket letters' belonging to Mary, Queen of Scots, and they were said to concern the murder of her second husband, Lord Darnley, who died in 1567. The letters were produced as evidence before tribunals held in London and York by the Earl of Morton. The validity of the letters was always suspect, and they went missing in 1584.

[*Century 8, quatrain 23*]

1568

La grande Royne quand se verra vaincue
Fera excez de masculin courage;
Sur cheval fleuve passera toute nué,
Suitte par fer, à soy fera outrage.

When the great Queen shall see herself defeated, she shall display enormous masculine courage. Riding naked on a horse she shall pass over the river. Pursued by iron, she shall have outraged her faith.

In May 1568, Mary, Queen of Scots, was forced to flee to England, having been defeated for the second time by the forces of the Earl of Murray at Carberry Hill. Her only possessions in her ignominious flight were the clothes she stood up in (the reference to 'nakedness'). She crossed over the River Tweed in a ferryboat but then continued her journey south on horseback. Mary's scandalous affair with the Earl of Bothwell, the probable murderer of her husband, Lord Darnley, and her subsequent marriage to Bothwell, had caused outrage among her fellow Catholics and Scots in general. By her behaviour, Mary severely tried the patience and loyalty of her supporters and subjects.

[*Century 1, quatrain 86*]

Quand ceux d'Hinault, de Gand & de Bruxelles
Verront à Langres le siege deuant mis,
Derriere leurs flancs seront guerres cruelles,
La pluye antique, fera pis qu'ennemys.

When those of Hainault, Ghent and Brussels shall see a siege laid before Langres; behind their flanks there will be cruel wars, the former wound being worse than their enemies.

This quatrain refers to the siege of the city of Langres during the Hapsburg Wars, although it is not certain to which incident the 'former wound' alludes.

[*Century 2, quatrain 50*]

1569 onwards

Chassez seront sans faire long combat,
Par le pays seront plus fort grevez;
Bourg & Cité auront plus grand debat.
Carcas, Narbonne auront cœurs esprouvez.

They will be driven away for an extended conflict. Those in the countryside will be greatly troubled. The town and the city shall have a great debate, and Carcassone and Narbonne will prove their heart.

Here is foretold the conflict that affected southern France for over thirty years—from 1562 to 1598. It involved the Catholics and the Huguenots (French Protestants), and in this conflict the town of Carcassone supported the Catholics but the Huguenots gained part of it. As often happened in such conflicts, there was a struggle for superiority between the aristocratic families who each took a particular religious stance. In the end, Henri IV acceded to the throne but only by changing his religion, from Protestantism to Catholicism.

[*Century 1, quatrain 5*]

1569

Bossu sera esleu par le conseil,
Plus hydeux monstre en terre n'aperceu;
Le coup volant prelat crevera l'œil,
Le traistre au Roy pour fidelle receu.

The hunchback shall be elected by the council, a more hideous monster upon earth was never seen. The deliberate shot shall puncture his eye, the traitor to the king received as faithful.

This quatrain is believed to refer to the hunchbacked Prince Louis de Condé, who was elected as leader of the Huguenot Council in 1560. In spite of the fact that he made public protestations of loyalty to King Charles IX in 1560 and 1562, he was secretly plotting against him. In March 1569, Condé was captured during the Battle of Jarnac and was intentionally shot in the head, even although he was a prisoner, as a punishment for his treachery.

[*Century 3, quatrain 41*]

1571

Au port Selin le tyran mis à mort,
La liberté non pourtant recouvree
Le nouveau Mars par vindicte & remort,
Dame par la foere de frayeur honoree.

At the port the tyrant Selim shall be put to death, but liberty shall not be recovered. The new war begins out of vengeance and remorse. A lady is honoured by force of fear.

1571

This refers to the defeat of the Turks by Christian forces at the Battle of Lepanto in October 1571. Although the Sultan Selim II was not killed, his naval commander, Ali Pasha, met his death on board ship. Turkish aggression around the Mediterranean ceased as a result of the battle, but it was several hundred years before freedom from the Ottoman influence was regained. The Pope decreed that the victory at Lepanto was due to the miraculous influence of the Virgin Mary, and this is referred to in the last line of the quatrain.

[*Century 1, quatrain 94*]

> *La barbe crespe & noire par engin,*
> *Subjuguera la gent cruelle & fiere;*
> *Le grand Chyren ostera du longin,*
> *Tous les captifs par Seline baniere.*

The frizzy and black beard by conflict will subjugate the nation cruel and proud. The great Chiren will take from far off all the captives by Seline's banner.

This quatrain is usually attributed to the Battle of Lepanto, which took place in 1571, five years after Nostradamus died. Don John of Austria ('the frizzy and black beard') was the commander of the Christian forces who defeated the Turkish warriors ('the nation cruel and proud'). 'Chiren' is held to be an anagram of Henric and refers to Henri III, who became King of France in 1574. The Battle of Lepanto freed many Christian captives who were being forced to man the ships of the Turkish fleet.

[*Century 2, quatrain 79*]

> *De Barcelonne, de Gennes & Venise,*
> *De la Secille pres Monaco unis*
> *Contre Barbare classe prendront la vise,*
> *Barbar poulsé bien loing jusqu'à Thunis.*

From Barcelona, from Genoa and Venice, from Sicily near Monaco, united against the Barbarian fleet they will take aim, the Barbarians will be driven back as far as Tunis.

In October 1571 was the Battle of Lepanto, an event that matches this quatrain well. In that battle, the Turks were defeated by an alliance of the papacy, Venice and Spain. The Turkish fleet comprised in large part the ships of their Algerian allies. Tunis was eventually captured two years after this battle.

[*Century 9, quatrain 42*]

1572

Le noir farouche quand aura essayé,
Sa main sanguine par feu, fer, arcs tendus,
Trestout le peuple sera tant effrayé,
Voir les plus grands par col & pieds pendus.

The wild ferocious king shall have tried his bloody hand by fire, the sword and bended bows. All the people shall be so afraid of seeing the great ones hanging by the neck and feet.

The 'ferocious king' referred to in these lines is usually thought to be Charles IX of France, who was reputed to be bloodthirsty on the hunting field, given to cutting off the heads of animals. People were terrified because of the slaughter, on St Bartholomew's Day, of many French Protestants (24 August 1572). Catherine de' Medici, alarmed at the growing influence of the Protestant Huguenots with Charles, her son, abetted her third son, Henri (later Henri III), in the instigation of the slaughter, which was timed to coincide with the marriage of her daughter, Margaret of Valois, to Henri of Navarre (later Henri IV). The Huguenot leader, Admiral Coligny, was one of the first to be put to death by an unruly mob. He was hung up by the foot so that his body could be abused by the people. This incident took place only a few years after Nostradamus' own death.

[*Century 4, quatrain 47*]

1572–1584

Le circuit du grand fait ruyneux,
Au nom septiesme le cinquiesme sera;
D'un tiers plus grand l'estrange belliqueux
Mouton, Lutece, Aix garantira.

The circuit of the great, disastrous action ruined, the name of the seventh shall be that of the fifth. Of the third, a much greater, foreign, warlike man, Aries shall not keep Paris and Aix.

This quatrain refers to the seven offspring of Catherine de' Medici, particularly Henri III, her third son and fifth child, who became the seventh and final Valois King of France. Great conflict had broken out from the 1560s onwards between Catholics and Protestants. Catherine de' Medici, as Regent, favoured a moderate approach with some religious freedom, but the more extreme Catholic faction wanted all Protestantism to be stamped out. There were massacres of Protestants, especially in 1572 when over 3,000 were murdered on St Bartholomew's Day ('the great, disastrous action'). This had grave repercussions for Henri III, who was neither in favour with the militant Catholics nor the Protestants. He was assassinated by the monk, Jacques Clément, in 1589 (*see* Century 1, quatrain 97, page 48). Catherine's daughter, Margaret of Valois, had married the Protestant Henri, Prince of Navarre ('the greater, foreign, warlike man'). He became heir to the throne of France (becoming Henri IV) but did not succeed without conflict. During March and April (under the sign of Aries), he began the siege of Paris and was finally accepted by France. He brought the religious wars to an end by becoming a

Catholic himself and by issuing the Edict of Nantes, which allowed freedom of worship to the Protestants. (The numbers III and IV added together also make the seven referred to in the quatrain.)

[*Century 2, quatrain 88*]

Aux temples, saints seront faits grands scandales,
Comptez seront par honneur & louanges,
D'un que l'on graué d'argent, d'or les medalles,
La fin sera en tourmens bien estranges.

In the sacred temples great scandals shall be committed, that shall be accounted as honours and praiseworthy. By one whom they engrave on silver, gold and medals, the end of it shall be in very strange torments.

The Huguenot Henri of Navarre was the leader of the Protestants in France and was detested by Nostradamus, a devout Catholic. As King of Navarre, he had money and medals struck bearing the image of his own head, and this currency was used in churches ('great scandals', which are counted as 'praiseworthy'). The 'strange torments' at the end of it all may be the massacre of 3,000 Protestants on St Bartholomew's Day, 1572, in Paris. Henri became heir (later Henri IV) in 1584 and went on to embrace the Catholic faith and to proclaim the Edict of Nantes, which gave religious freedom to the Protestants. These measures brought about a short-term peace.

[*Century 6, quatrain 9*]

1573

La pestilence l'entour de Capadille,
Une autre faim pres de Sagone s'appreste;
Le chevalier bastard de bon senille,
Au grand de Thunes fera trancher la teste.

1574

The plague is around Capellades, another famine shall approach Sagunto. The knightly bastard of the good old man shall cause the great one of Tunis to lose his head.

This quatrain refers to the recapture of Tunis by Don John of Austria in 1573. He was the illegitimate son of Charles V and took the city for Philip II of Spain, his half-brother. There had been periodic outbreaks of plague in this area, and those affected by the illness were not able to eat.

[*Century 8, quatrain 50*]

1574

Par lors qu'un Roy sera contre les siens,
Natif de Bloys subjuguera Ligures;
Mammel, Cordube & les Dalmatiens,
Des sept puis l'ombre à Roy estrennes & lemures.

At a time when a king is against his own, native of Blois he will subjugate the league. Mammel, Cordoba and the Dalmatians, of the seven a shadow to the king, money and spirits of the dead.

This quatrain probably describes Henri III of France, a descendant of the house of Blois and third child of Catherine de Medici, who will subjugate the Catholic League. The seven children of Catherine are referred to along with hints of intrigue, money changing hands and unquiet death—all factors very common at that time.

[*Century 10, quatrain 44*]

1574–1584

Deux Royals freres si fort guerroyeront,
Qu'entre 'eux sera la guerre si mortelle,
Qu'un chacun places fortes occuperont,
De regne & vie sera leur grand querelle.

Two royal brothers will wage such strong war against each other and the fight between them shall be so mortal that each of them will occupy fortified places. The kingdom and life shall be concerned in their great quarrel.

This quatrain describes the relationship and state of affairs between Henri III of France and his brother, François, Duke of Alençon (later Duke of Anjou), in the years 1574–1584. François took leadership of the Huguenots while Henri allied himself with the Catholic League. François proposed marriage to Elizabeth I of England but was refused. On François's death in 1584, Henri of Navarre succeeded as heir to Henri III.

[*Century 3, quatrain 98*]

1575–1589

Des sept rameaux à trois seront reduits,
Les plus aisnez seront surprins par mort.
Fratricider les deux seront seduits,
Les conjurez en dormant seront morts.

The seven branches shall be reduced to three, the older ones will be surprised by death, two of them will be attracted towards fratricide, the conspirators shall die in their sleep.

This is an accurate quatrain describing the children of Catherine de' Medici ('the seven branches'). By 1575, only three of them were still alive—Henri III, François, Duke of Alençon, and Margaret of Valois, wife of Henri de Navarre. The two brothers were great rivals and plotted against each other. Henri III ordered the assassination of the de Guise brothers. François had been in league with the family de Guise in the hope of ousting his brother from the throne, hence both were 'attracted to fratricide'. François and Margaret died in their beds (the latter in 1615), but Henri III was assassinated by the monk, Jacques Clément.

[*Century 6, quatrain 11*]

1577

Pour le plaisir d'edict voluptueux,
On meslera la poison dans la loy;
Venus sera en cours si vertueux,
Qu'offusquera du Soleil tout aloy.

For the pleasure of a voluptuous edict, poison shall be mixed with the law; Venus shall be still so virtuous that all the alloy of the sun shall be obscured.

In this quatrain, Nostradamus foretells the publication of the Edict of Poitiers in 1577, ten years after his own death. This edict allowed freedom of worship for Calvinists and relaxed the prohibition preventing clergy from marrying. Nostradamus strongly disapproved of this and believed that it encouraged depravity. The court of Henri III was certainly notorious, having a reputation for promiscuity and extravagance. The king himself was a homosexual, and this caused outrage among some of his subjects, as did his reputation for dabbling in sorcery and magic.

[*Century 5, quatrain 72*]

1580

Celuy qu'aura tant d'honneur & caresses,
A son entrée en la Gaule Belgique,
Un temps apres fera tant de rudesses,
Et sera contre à la fleur tant bellique.

He who shall have had so much honour and welcome at his entry into French Belgium, a short time after shall commit so many rudenesses and shall be against the flower so warlike.

François, Duke of Alençon, was sent by his brother, Henri III, King of France, to be governor of the Netherlands, and this was in accordance with the wishes of the people. They had invited François to be their protector, and he was welcomed into the region. Apparently, he became captivated by the wealth and grandeur of the city of Antwerp and attempted to capture the city by force. He was soundly defeated by the people of the city, and many of his soldiers were killed. By this selfish and ill-judged act, he lost all credibility and was no longer trusted by the people.

[*Century 6, quatrain 83*]

De plus grand perte nouvelles rapportees,
Le rapport fait le camp s'eslongnera;
Bendes unies encontre revoltees,
Double phalange grand abandonnera.

News is brought of the great loss, the report revealed will astonish the camp. Bands unite against those engaged in revolt, the double phalanx will abandon the great one.

This quatrain is usually attributed to an event that affected the Duke of Parma's army in 1580. The soldiers were alarmed by the spread of a rumour—news of a great defeat elsewhere.

There was considerable confusion, which allowed the Dutch forces that they were fighting briefly to regain control of Antwerp. Two phalanxes of men (two times 800, hence 1,600) revolted and turned against their compatriots.

[*Century 4, quatrain 13*]

1582

Dans deux logis de nuict le feu prendra,
Plusieurs dedans estouffez & rostis,
Pres de deux fleuves pour seur il adviendra
Sol, l'Arc & Caper, tous seront amortis.

In two houses at night the fire shall take hold, many people inside will be suffocated and burnt. Near two rivers it shall come to pass for sure when the sun, Sagittarius and Capricorn are all mortified.

A fire with severe consequences has occurred or perhaps is still to take place within two houses in a town beside two rivers. The prediction was connected with a fire that occurred in Lyons in December 1582, by contemporary commentators of that time. Each year, on 22 December, the sun moves into Capricorn from Sagittarius.

[*Century 2, quatrain 35*]

1584

Le rang Lorrain fera place à Vandosme,
Le haut mis bas, & le bas mis en haut,
Le fils d'Hamon sera esleu dans Rome,
Et les deux grands seront mis en defaut.

1584

The house of Lorraine will give place to Vendôme, the high put low and the low put on high, the son of Harion will be elected in Rome, and the two great ones will be put at fault.

This quatrain fits very well with the rise of Henri IV, the Duke of Vendôme, otherwise known as Henri of Navarre. Around the 1560s, the French Wars of Religion broke out, with the Catholics and Huguenots (the name given to the French Protestants) each perpetrating barbaric acts. In 1572 around 3,000 Huguenots were killed in Paris, and in 1599 the king was thrown out by extreme Catholics. The more moderate Catholics were led by Catherine de' Medici. In 1584, the Huguenot Henri became heir to the throne. He was able to end the war by becoming a Catholic and therefore acceptable in the eyes of Rome ('will be elected in Rome'). He made an agreement with his Protestant supporters (in the Edict of Nantes) that allowed them freedom of worship in much of the country. The two great ones 'put at fault' (alternatively translated as 'at a loss' or 'shall not appear') are the Duke de Guise and the Duke de Mayenne.
[*Century 10, quatrain 18*]

L'ombre du regne de Navarre non vray,
Fera la vie de sort illegitime;
La veu promis incertain de Cambray,
Roy d'Orleans donra mur legitime.

The shadow of the reign of Navarre is not true, it will make the life of illegitimate fate. The uncertain allowance from Cambrai, King of Orleans will give a lawful wall.

This quatrain seems to refer also to Henri of Navarre, who became heir to the French throne in 1584. The shadow of the reign could refer to the fact that he had not gained a hold on the whole of France, referring possibly to the large areas and certain fortified cities in which the Huguenots were left to their own devices, outside royal control. Henri led a far from ordinary life, with many mistresses, including the wife of the Governor of Cambrai. By way of return, Henri gave hereditary possession of the town to the family.

[*Century 10, quatrain 45*]

1585–1589

Quand chef Perousse n'osera sa tunique,
Sens au couvert tout nud s'expolier,
Seront print sept faict aristocratique,
Le pere & fils morts par points au collier.

When the chief of Perouse shall not dare to risk his tunic, without his cover to be exposed quite naked; then shall be taken seven aristocrats, the father and son dead by a stab through the collar.

The 'chief of Perouse' is the Pope, referring in this quatrain to Pope Sextus V. He had been forced to excommunicate Henri of Navarre in 1585 and found himself facing the same possibility with Henri III. He was unwilling to do so because he risked alienating the whole of France and losing more revenue for the papacy. (Sweden and England had already severed links with the Roman Church, in 1527 and 1530 respectively, resulting in a considerable loss of income for the Catholic Church.) Hence the Pope did not 'dare to risk his tunic and be exposed quite naked', but in 1589 he found that he had no other option. The 'seven aristocrats' are the family of Catherine de' Medici. Catherine's husband and father of their seven children, Henri II of France, had been killed by an accidental stab wound in the throat. Their son, Henri III, was killed in 1589 by the fanatical Dominican monk, Jacques Clément, although the fatal stab wound was in the stomach rather than the throat (*see* Century 1, quatrain 97, page 48).

[*Century 5, quatrain 67*]

1588

Tard le Monarque se viendra repentir,
De n'avoir mis à mort son adversaire,
Mais viendra bien à plus haut consentir,
Que tout son sang par mort fera deffaire.

The monarch shall repent too late that he did not put his rival to death. But he will soon give his consent to a far greater thing, that all his line will die.

The likeliest interpretation here is that it refers to Henri III and his obsession that he eliminate the Guise family from French politics. He ordered the assassination of the Duke of Guise and his brother, Louis, in December, 1588, but the third brother, the Duke of Mayenne, was allowed to survive. In fact, he was the leader of the conspiracy, and Henri was eventually forced to take further action in this respect.

[*Century 1, quatrain 36*]

Par la response de dame, Roy troublé,
Ambassadeurs mespriseront leur vie,
Le grand ses freres contrefera doublé,
Par deux mourront ire, haine, envie.

The king is troubled by the woman's answer. Ambassadors shall be contemptuous of their lives. The greater of his brothers will doubly counterfeit. Two shall die due to anger, hatred and envy.

This has been attributed to the murder of the Duke of Guise and his brother, Louis, the Cardinal of Lorraine, at Blois shortly before Christmas in 1588. They were assassinated by a member of the royal bodyguard on the orders of King Henri III because he was fearful of the political power that was commanded by the powerful duke and his family. The king's mother, Catherine de' Medici, was extremely angry with her son because of these murders. The surviving brother of the Duke of Guise, the Duke of Mayenne, went on to wield enormous power in France as lieutenant-general and leader of the Catholic League (the 'doubly counterfeit' referred to in the quatrain).

[*Century 1, quatrain 85*]

> *La republique de la grande Cité*
> *A grand rigueur ne voudra consentir;*
> *Roy sortir hors par trompette cité,*
> *L'eschelle au mur la cité repentir.*

The government of the people of the great city will not consent to severe repression. The king summoned by trumpets to leave the city, the ladder at the wall, the city shall repent.

On 12 May 1588, the Catholic League assumed power in Paris in the name of its citizens. This followed the Journée des Barricades ('Day of the Barricades'), when the people had forced King Henri III and his supporters to flee from the city. Henri's response was to join forces with Henri of Navarre, who was married to Henri III's sister, Margaret of Valois. They met at St Cloud and plotted together to recapture Paris. Before this plan could come to fruition, however, King Henri was assassinated by the monk, Jacques Clément.

[*Century 3, quatrain 50*]

> *Paris conjure un grand meurtre commettre*
> *Blois le fera sortir en plain effect;*
> *Ceux d'Orleans voudront leur chef remettre,*
> *Angiers, Troye, Langres leur feront grand forfait.*

Paris conspires to commit a great murder, Blois shall make sure that it is completely carried out. The people of Orléans

will want to put back their leader. Angers, Troyes and Langres will commit a misdemeanour against them.

These lines refer to the assassination of Henri, Duke of Guise, and his brother, Louis, the Cardinal of Lorraine, who were murdered in December 1588 on the orders of King Henri III. Henri III had long been in rivalry with the powerful duke, who himself had ambitions for the throne of France. This conflict had occurred over leadership of the Catholic League, which was set up by the duke in 1568, although the king had attempted to assume control. Henri feared that the duke was becoming ever more powerful, and so ordered his assassination, which was carried out by one of the royal bodyguard. On the following day, 24 December, the cardinal met a similar fate, and both were murdered in Blois. Immediately after these events, the outraged people of Orléans staged a revolt and threw out their governor, Balzac d'Entragues. He was replaced by a powerful member of the Catholic League, a man of proven loyalty to the murdered duke, Charles de Lorraine. Nostradamus is not correct in the last line of this quatrain, as Angers and Langres were supporters of the League while Troyes did not swear allegiance to either side. In the following year, 1589, Henri III was himself assassinated at St Cloud by the monk, Jacques Clément. (*See also* Century 1, quatrain 85, pages 45–46.)

[*Century 3, quatrain 51*]

1589

Ce que fer, flamme, n'a sceu paracheuer,
La douce langue au conseil viendra faire
Par repos, songe, le Roy fera resuer,
Plus l'ennemy en feu, sang militaire.

That which neither fire nor weapon could accomplish shall be brought about by a soft tongue in council. In sleep and dreaming, the king shall more see the enemy, not in war or military blood.

This quatrain alludes to the assassination of King Henri III of France in 1589 by a monk called Jacques Clément. The king had a premonition of his death three days before the event, when he dreamed that he saw his royal cloak and accoutrements being trampled underfoot by monks and the general population. The monk, Jacques Clément, approached the king at a meeting of the council at St Cloud. Saying that he was the bearer of a confidential letter, he leaned over as though to communicate its contents and stabbed the king in his stomach. Henri was not killed outright but died the following day.

[*Century 1, quatrain 97*]

1590

Combien de fois prinse Cité solaire,
Seras, changeant les lois barbares & vaines
Ton mal s'approche, plus seras tributaire,
Le grand Hadrie recouvrira tes veines.

How many times will you be taken, O city of the sun? Changing the barbaric and vain laws. Great evil approaches you. You will be more tributary. The great Hadrie will recover your veins.

Much of this quatrain depends upon the translation of one or two words. One interpretation is that the 'city of the sun' refers to Paris, which was under siege by the forces of Henri IV before he entered it in 1590. The 'barbaric' laws were probably those of the revolutionary group that governed Paris. The siege of Paris lasted for six months. If Hadrie is taken as meaning Henri, then the last line probably reflects Henri's actions in passing food to the starving people of Paris.

The context changes with alternative meanings. The 'city of the sun' could be an ancient city in Syria, and if Hadrie is read as Adrie then the last line would refer to the great Venice. (*See also* Century 1, quatrain 9, page 30.)

[*Century 1, quatrain 8*]

1591

Esleu en Pape, d'esleu sera mocqué,
Subit soudain esmeu prompt & timide,
Par trop bon doux à mourir provoqué,
Crainte estainte la nuit de sa mort guide.

Elected as Pope once elected, he will be mocked, suddenly moved promptly and timid, by too much goodness provoked to die, his fear present on the night of his death a guide.

Cardinal Santa Severina was elected Pope following the death of Pope Gregory XIV but he was deposed and the election was declared illegal and he died, it is said of grief, two months later in 1591. His successor did not fare much better as he also died within two months of election.

[*Century 10, quatrain 12*]

1594

Dans le conflit le grand qui peu valloit
A son dernier fera cas merveilleux :
Pendant qu'Hadrie verra ce qu'il falloit,
Dans le banquet pongnale l'orgueilleux.

1594

In the conflict the great man who is of little worth, at his last trial shall do a marvellous feat. While Hadrie sees what is needed, in the banquet he stabs the proud ones.

In France in 1594, the Catholic League was becoming increasingly alarmed at the activities of the People's Parliament and feared losing control. The Duke of Mayenne, surviving brother of the powerful de Guise family (*see* Century 1, quatrain 85, pages 45–46), invited all the leaders of the League to a banquet. On the duke's orders they were all slaughtered during the festivities. The duke, who was the head of the Catholic League and who had a claim to the throne of France, hoped to further his own position by this move. However, Henri IV (Hadrie) realized that in order to save the situation and unite the people behind him, he must himself convert to the Catholic faith.

[*Century 2, quatrain 55*]

Qui au royaume Navarrois parviendra,
Quand le Sicile & Naples seront joints,
Bigorre & Landes par Foix lorran tiendra,
D'un qui d'Espagne sera par trop conjoints.

He that shall inherit the kingdom of the Navarre. When Sicily and Naples shall be joined, he shall hold Bigorre and Landes by Foix and Oloron from one who will be too much in league with Spain.

These lines refer to Henri, Prince of Navarre, who became King Henri IV of France in 1594. The person 'too much in league with Spain' may be Philip of Spain's wife, Elizabeth, daughter of Henri II of France and Navarre's own cousin.

[*Century 3, quatrain 25*]

1596

De Barcelone par mer si grande armee
Toute Marseille de frayeur tremblera,
Isles saisies, de mer ayde fermee,
Ton traditeur en terre nagera.

From Barcelona such a great army will come by sea, all Marseilles shall tremble with fear. The islands seized, and shut off by sea, your traitor will swim on land.

On 17 February 1596, the King of Spain, Philip II, sent ships to blockade Marseilles. They commanded the approaches to the port by anchoring near, and seizing, the islands of Chateau d'If and Ratonneau. Marseilles continued to hold out, but a traitor, Charles de Caseau, plotted to betray Marseilles to the enemy. His plans were discovered, and he died by an assassin's sword. His lungs filled with blood so that he drowned. Nostradamus may have been thinking of this event when he wrote 'your traitor will swim on land'.

[*Century 3, quatrain 88*]

Devant le lac où plus cher fut getté
De sept mois, & son ost desconfit
Seront Hispans par Albannois gastez,
Par delay perte en donnant le conflit.

In front of the lake where the treasure was cast, for seven months and his army discomfited. Spaniards shall be spoiled by those of Alba, by delaying in giving battle, loss.

This quatrain is thought to refer to the attack on forty Spanish galleons, laden with gold and treasure, in the Bay of Cadiz in 1596. The attack was carried out by the British fleet, led by the Earls of Essex and Howard and Sir Walter Raleigh. The Spanish vessels were returning from a seven months' voyage to South America and had dropped anchor in the Bay of Cadiz ('lake'—the word *gaddir*, from which Cadiz is derived, means 'an enclosed space'). The bay is entered through a narrow neck of water, and the Spanish had thought that they were safe, even although they had earlier spotted the English fleet on the open sea. Hence the attack when it came was something of a surprise, and the Spanish scuttled their ships rather than allow the treasure to fall into English hands. When Nostradamus wrote this quatrain, England and Spain were allies because Henry VIII's daughter, Mary Tudor, was the wife of the Spanish king, Philip II.

[*Century 8, quatrain 94*]

1599–1658

Plus Macelin que Roy en Angleterre,
Lieu obscur nay par force aura l'empire.
Lasche sans foy sans loy seignera terre.
Son temps s'approche si pres que je souspire.

More of a butcher than a king of England, born in obscurity but by force he shall gain an empire. Coward, without faith, without law he shall bleed the land; his time is approaching so close that I sigh.

In this verse, Nostradamus is referring to the life and times of Oliver Cromwell, who was born thirty years after his own death. Nostradamus thoroughly disliked Cromwell, who was indeed born of humble origins and who, as a Protestant, was a heretic 'without faith', as far as the devout Catholic seer was concerned. Cromwell is called a 'butcher' because of the bloodshed of the English Civil War and the examples that were made of some civilians (*see* Century 5, quatrain 60, page 65).

[*Century 8, quatrain 76*]

1599–1658 or 1769–1821

De soldat simple parviendra en empire,
De robe courte parviendra à la longue
Vaillant aux armes en eglise ou plus pyre,
Vexer les prestres comme l'eau faict l'esponge.

From simple soldier he shall come to have an empire, from a short robe he shall come to have a long one. Valiant in arms, no worse man towards the church, he shall vex the priests as water soaks into a sponge.

This verse applies equally well to the life and career of either Oliver Cromwell or Napoleon Bonaparte, both of whom caused considerable problems for the Church.

[*Century 8, quatrain 57*]

1601

L'œil de Ravenne sera destitué,
Quand à ses pieds les aisles sailliront,
Les deux de Bresse auront constitué,
Turin, Verseil, que Gaulois fouleront.

The eye of Ravenna will be destitute, when the wings will rise to his feet. The two of Bresse shall have constituted Turin and Vercelli, which the French will have trod upon.

This quatrain can be seen to refer to several instances of occupation by the French, spread over many years but occurring initially with the possession of Bresse in 1601. Turin was occupied in 1640 and again from 1798 for almost twenty years, while Vercelli was taken in 1704 and again, also in 1798. Ravenna (in

53

north-eastern Italy), which was one of the papal states, did not suffer the same fate but presumably looked upon the subjugation of these places with trepidation.

[*Century 1, quatrain 6*]

1604–1607

La grand Bretagne comprinse d'Angleterre,
Viendra par eaux si fort à inonder .
La ligue neufue d'Ausonne fera guerre,
Que contre eux il se viendra bander.

Great Britain, including England will be inundated by deep flooding. The new league in Ausonne will make war so that they will band against them.

Great Britain did not come into existence until 1604, forty years after the death of Nostradamus and so his use of the title is an interesting one, predicting the union of the crowns of England and Scotland under James I in 1601. In 1607, there was widespread flooding in south-west England, in Somerset and in the area around Bristol, and this seems to have been accurately foreseen. 'Ausonne' stands for Italy, and in 1606 there was a renewal of the Holy League to which many were opposed.

[*Century 3, quatrain 70*]

1607

Croistra le nombre si grand des Astronomes
Chassez, bannis & livres censurez,
L'an mil six cens & sept par sacre glomes,
Que nul aux sacres ne seront assurez.

The number of astrologers shall grow so great that they shall be driven out, banished and books censored. In the year 1607 by sacred assemblies, so that the safety of none shall be assured from the holy ones.

The Roman Catholic Church viewed astrology with alarm and suspicion, and, in the year 1607, Pope Urban VIII banned a particularly influential book, *Dekkers' Almanac*. Those found with the book in their possession risked excommunication from the Church, and this action caused a great deal of controversy. Although this particular event occurred after his death, Nostradamus, who was a devout and fervent Catholic, had himself experienced difficulties with the Church because of his interest in astrology. In fact, banning *Dekkers' Almanac* merely served to drive the book 'underground' and make it even more influential, as, throughout history, has often proved to be the case when material is censored.

[*Century 8, quatrain 71*]

1610

Les armes battre au ciel longue saison,
L'arbre au milieu de la cité tombé,
Vermine, rongne, glaive en face tyfon,
Lors le Monarque d'Hadrie succombé.

The weapons fight in the sky for a long while, the tree falls in the middle of the city. The sacred branch destroyed, a sword in front of Tison, then the king of Hadrie succumbs.

The first line of this quatrain appears to indicate that Nostradamus predicted twentieth-century aerial warfare. However, 'Hadrie' is normally taken to refer to Henri IV of France, and the rest of this verse fits well with the assassination of the king in May 1610. In this context, the first line may allude to a ghostly army that was reported to have been seen in the sky at the time of the murder. Henri is described as 'the sacred branch' because he was anointed as king when he succeeded to the throne. He received a fatal stab wound from a religious fanatic near the Rue Tison in Paris and was the 'tree that falls in the middle of the city'.

[*Century 3, quatrain 11*]

Par les contrees du grand fleuve Bethique
Loing d'Ibere au royaume de Grenade,
Croix repoussees par gens Mahometiques,
Un de Cordobe trahyra la contrade.

Through the countries of the great River Guadalquivir, far off from Spain to the kingdom of Grenada. The cross repulsed by the Mohammedans, one from Cordova shall betray his country.

Grenada, a Moorish stronghold, was captured by Spain in 1492. Numbers of Jewish people who lived in these lands were allowed to remain in their homes and businesses provided that they embraced Christianity. Later, in 1610, the Jews were persecuted and forced to flee from Spain in spite of the fact that a treaty to safeguard their position had been negotiated by one Gonsalvo Fernandez de Cordova.

[*Century 3, quatrain 20*]

1615

L'enfant Royal contemnera la mere,
Oeil, pieds blessez, rude, inobeissant,
Nouvelle à dame estrange & bien amere,
Seront tuez des siens plus de cinq cens.

The royal child shall scorn his mother; eye, feet wounded, rude, disobedient. News to the lady is strange and bitter, there shall be killed more than five hundred of her people.

This quatrain describes the relationship between Louis XIII and his mother, Marie de' Medici. In 1615, the advisers of the fifteen-year-old king persuaded him to take up arms against his mother, who was regent at that time. About five hundred of the queen's soldiers were killed.

[*Century 7, quatrain 11*]

1618–1648

Par grand fureur le Roy Romain Belgique,
Vexer voudra par phalange barbare.
Fureur grinçant chassera gent Lybique,
Depuis Pannons jusques Hercules la hare.

By great fury the Roman king will wish to vex Belgium by barbarian soldiers. In gnashing fury he will chase the savage people from Hungary as far as Gibraltar.

This quatrain appears to describe events in the Thirty Years' War. The 'Roman king' is Ferdinand II, the Holy Roman Emperor, a devout and fervent Catholic soldier who dreamed of seeing a Catholic Germany. However, the forces ranged against him were strong—Denmark, Sweden, Norway, Saxony and Brandenburg in the north, the Ottoman Empire in the south, and German Protestants in the west around the Rhine. Russia and Poland posed an additional threat. Eventually, Ferdinand united with the Catholic Hapsburgs of Spain under King Philip IV, but the resulting conflict ruined and devastated Germany. The Treaties of Westphalia, drawn up in 1648, recognized the sovereignty of the United Netherlands and

1625–1649 or 1810–1814

Le divin mal surprendra le grand Prince,
Un peu devant aura femme espousee.
Son puy & credit à un coup viendra mince,
Conseil mourra pour la teste rasee.

The divine wrath surprises the great prince a little while before his marriage to a woman. His support and credit all at once becomes slim; Council, he shall die for the shaven head.

This quatrain may be open to two interpretations, the first referring to the troubled reign of Charles I, King of Great Britain and Ireland, and his eventual execution in 1649. In 1625, Charles married the Catholic princess, Henrietta Maria of France, and on his wedding day ordered that all persecution of Catholics should cease. Parliament was already angry because of the arrogance of the king and refused to give its support. At the same time, a request for more money to fund the war in Spain was refused (support and credit). Charles dissolved parliament and only recalled it in 1640 because he had run out of money. By 1642, the situation had deteriorated to such an extent that the Civil War broke out between Charles and his Royalists and the supporters of parliament, the Roundheads, led by Oliver Cromwell. Charles was sentenced to death by the council he had formed, as was demanded by the victorious Roundheads (shaven heads).

Another interpretation of this quatrain may be the divorce by Emperor Napoleon of Josephine and his subsequent marriage to Austrian archduchess, Marie Louise, in 1810. This caused outrage among many of his former supporters and also with Pope Pius VII, who ordered Napoleon's excommunication (the 'shaven head' referred to in the quatrain). There were scenes of rejoicing when a son was born to Napoleon in 1811, but he then embarked upon the Russian campaign which brought about his downfall.

[*Century 1, quatrain 88*]

1627

De l'archeduc d'Uticense, Gardoing,
Par la forest & mont inaccessible,
En my du pont sera tasché au poing,
Le chef Nemans qui tant sera terrible.

Of the aqueduct of Uzès and Gard, by the forest and inaccessible mountains; in the middle of the bridge he will be tied by the fist, the chief of Nîmes who shall be very terrible.

This quatrain describes the siege of the Protestants of Nîmes in 1627. The Duke of Rohan moved his army to aid the city along the ancient Roman aqueduct, the Pont du Gard, which ran from Uzès to Nimes. Some structural work was needed so that the canons and other equipment could be moved forward. This military manoeuvre was successful, and the Duke was placed in charge ('chief of Nîmes') when he reached the town.

[*Century 5, quatrain 58*]

1632–1633

Le lys Dauffois portera dans Nansi,
Jusques en Flandres Electeur de l'Empire,
Neufue obturée au grand Montmorency,
Hors lieux provez delivre à clere peyne.

The Dauphin shall carry the lily into Nancy. As far as Flanders shall the Elector of the empire (be taken). New obstruction to great Montmorency, except for proved places, delivered to clear punishment.

The Dauphin who carried 'the lily into Nancy' was Louis XIII, who took the city in September 1633. In that year also, the Elector of the city of Trèves had been captured by the Spanish and taken to Flanders (now called Brussels). In 1632, Montmorency had attempted to lead a revolt against Louis XIII, but this had failed and he was taken prisoner. The petitions of his family failed to win him clemency but did succeed in gaining him a private execution rather than one in the public gaze. His head was chopped off in the courtyard of the prison rather than in the 'proved places' of public punishment.

[*Century 9, quatrain 18*]

1636

Aupres du Lac Leman sera conduite,
Par garse estrange cité voulant trahir,
Avant son meurtre à Aspurg la grand fuitte,
Et ceux du Rhin la viendront invahir.

Near Lake Geneva he will be conducted by a foreign woman who wants to betray the city. Before her death her great retinue will come to Augsburg, and those of the Rhine they shall come to invade.

This verse seems to relate to an event in the Thirty Years' War, the Battle of Augsburg. Defeat at this battle forced the army of Bernhard, Duke of Saxe Wiemar, to fall back across the Rhine. This allowed the Hapsburg armies of Ferdinand II to capture Augsburg and other towns on the River Rhine. The meaning of the reference to the foreign woman is not known.

[*Century 5, quatrain 12*]

1640

L'an que Mercure, Mars, Venus retrograde,
Du grand Monarque la ligne ne faillir,
Esleu du peuple l'usitant pres de Pactole,
Qu'en paix & regne viendra fort enviellir.

In the year that Mercury, Mars and Venus are retrograde, the family line of the great monarch shall not fail. Elected by the Portuguese people near Pactole and shall reign in peace for a good while.

This verse seems to describe the overthrow of the Spanish in Portugal and the reinstatement of a monarchy approved by the Portuguese people. Philip II of Spain conquered Portugal and reigned there as king until 1621. He was succeeded by his son, Philip III, but in 1640 the Portuguese revolted and threw out the Spanish. They re-established their own 'monarchy' under the powerful family of Breganza.

[*Century 4, quatrain 97*]

1641–1649

Du regne Anglois l'indigne dechasser,
Le conseiller, par ire mis à feu.
Ses adherants iront si bas trasser,
Que le bastard sera demy receu.

From the English kingdom an unworthy man is chased. The counsellor through anger will be burnt. His followers will sink to such base depths that the bastard shall almost be received.

The 'unworthy man' referred to here is considered to be Charles I, who alienated his people and dissolved parliament for eleven years from 1629. War in Scotland and lack of money caused Charles to recall parliament in 1640, but the Civil War erupted in 1642. One of Charles's councillors, the Earl of Strafford, was beheaded in 1641 while another, Archbishop Laud, who is referred to in these lines, was burnt at the stake for treason in 1645. The 'followers' who 'sink to such base depths' are the Scots who betrayed the king to Cromwell. The king himself was executed in 1649. The 'bastard' or pretender is a reference to Cromwell, who assumed power without having any real right to do so.

[*Century 3, quatrain 80*]

1642–1643

Vieux Cardinal par le jeune deceu,
Hors de sa charge se verra desarmé,
Arles ne monstres double soit aperceu,
Et Liqueduct & le Prince embaumé.

The old cardinal by a young one deceived and shall find himself changed, disarmed out of his position. Arles do not show that the double is perceived and Liqueduct (Aqueduct) and the Prince embalmed.

In this verse, Nostradamus predicts the manner in which Cardinal Richelieu was ousted by his young successor, the Marquis de Cinq-Mars, who was twenty-two years old at the time. Richelieu was forced to resign, having lost the confidence of Louis XIII. In Arles, a copy of a treacherous document signed by Cinq-Mars and the king's brother, involving an agreement with Spain, came into his hands. He travelled to Paris to inform the king but was very ill and died shortly afterwards, in December 1642. Five months later Louis himself was dead and both corpses were embalmed.

[*Century 8, quatrain 68*]

1642–1649

Un coronel machine ambition,
Se saisira de la plus grande armée;
Contre son prince feinte invention,
Et descouvert sera sous sa ramée.

A colonel intrigues by his ambition, he shall seize the greater part of the army. Against his prince a false invention, he shall be discovered under his own flag.

The colonel in this verse is accepted by most commentators as being Oliver Cromwell, who took over the greater part of the army and fought the Royalist forces under his own flag. Although he was undoubtedly a man governed by strong convictions, who believed that the course he followed was the correct one, many would say he was false to his king. Cromwell's success undoubtedly led to the downfall and eventual execution of King Charles I.

[*Century 4, quatrain 62*]

1642–1658

Le grand criard sans honte audacieux,
Sera esle gouverneur de l'armee,
La hardiesse de son contentieux
Le pont rompu, Cité de peur pasmee.

The great orator, shameless and audacious, will be chosen as governor of the army. The boldness of his contention, the broken bridge, the city faint from fear.

'The great orator' referred to in this quatrain is Oliver Cromwell, who took control of the Parliamentary forces and, eventually, government of the country itself. The 'broken bridge' is believed to allude to the Yorkshire town of Pontefract (*pons fractus* in Latin). Pontefract was a Royalist stronghold and was besieged on two occasions during the Civil War.

[*Century 3, quatrain 81*]

Par teste rase viendra bien mal eslire,
Plus que sa charge ne porte passera;
Si grand fureur & rage fera dire,
Qu'à feu & sang tout sexe tranchera.

By those with the shaven heads he will be seen to have been badly elected, weighed down with a load he cannot carry; such great fury and dire rage he will exhibit that fire, blood and all sex will be cut to pieces.

This quatrain refers to the Roundheads ('shaven heads') who elected Oliver Cromwell as their leader. He could not be described as 'badly elected', in that he emerged victorious after the Civil War in England and later campaigns in Scotland and Ireland. It may perhaps mean that he had no right to be in charge since there was a monarch who was held to rule by divine right. Nostradamus states that Cromwell was weighed down by his responsibilities, and the historical record bears this out. Certainly Cromwell agonized over the execution of Charles I but saw no alternative. Cromwell believed that he had God on his side, but in his conquest of rebellious Ireland in 1649 he exhibited 'great fury and rage'. Men, women, clergymen and children were flogged and put to death with great cruelty, notably at Drogheda and Limerick. Cromwell later wrote that he had acted in the 'heat of action', as though regretting the atrocities. However, he also wrote that 'Truly I believe this bitterness will save much blood through the goodness of God'—a classic avowal that 'the end justifies the means'. Nostradamus appears to have been very accurate in his assessment of the nature and activities of Oliver Cromwell.

[*Century 5, quatrain 60*]

1643–1715 and 1715–1774

Par le rameau du vaillant personnage,
De France infirme par le pere infelice .
Honneurs, richesses, travail en son vieil age,
Pour avoir creu le conseil d'homme nice.

By the branch of a valiant person, of weakened France, because of the unhappy father. Honours, riches, labour in his old age, because he believed the council of a simple man.

1644–1648

Cœur, vigueur, gloire, le regne changera,
De tous points, contre ayant son adversaire,
Lors France enfance par mort subjugera,
Le grand regent sera lors plus contraire.

Heart, vigour and glory will change the kingdom, on all sides, its adversary is against it, then France shall be subject to a child through death, the great regent shall then be most contrary.

In these quatrains, reference is made to the glorious reign of King Louis XIV, who was known as Le Roi Soleil (the 'Sun King'). Born in 1638, he was five years old when he became heir to the throne but did not become king until 1660. During his minority, France was ruled by ministers. Throughout his reign, the king and the aristocracy were caught up in the glittering life of the court at Versailles. He was succeeded by Louis XV, who also became heir to the throne in childhood. All power in France was effectively placed in the hands of the regent, Philippe, Duke of Orléans. France became virtually bankrupt during Louis XV's reign, although the aristocracy retained enormous wealth which could not be touched by the nation ('weakened France'). This state of affairs eventually unleashed the forces of revolution, preceded by an attempted assassination of the king in 1757. 'Honours, riches, labour in his old age' is believed to be a reference to Fleury, the king's elderly tutor and priest, who became influential late in life at the age of seventy-two.

[*Century 3, quatrains 14 and 15*]

1644–1648

Quand Innocent tiendra le lieu de Pierre,
Le Nizaram Sicilian se verra,
En grands honneurs, mais apres il cherra,
Dans le bourbier d'une civil guerre.

When Innocent shall hold the place of Peter, the Sicilian Niazaram shall see himself in great honours, but after that he shall descend into the dirt of a civil war.

From the first line of this quatrain, it is possible to place it during the period when Pope Innocent X ('Peter') held office, and he was elected in 1644. The 'Sicilian Niazaram' is Cardinal Mazarin of France, an Italian by birth who rose to a position of great influence under the protection of his predecessor, Cardinal Richelieu. After Richelieu's death in 1643, Mazarin was responsible for the conduct of many of the affairs of France during the final period of the Thirty Years' War.

[*Century 7, quatrain 42*]

1648–1649

La forteresse aupres de la Tamise
Cherra par lors, le Roy dedans serré,
Aupres du pont sera veu en chemise
Un devant mort, puis dans le fort barré.

The fortress near the Thames shall fall when the king is imprisoned within. He shall be seen in his shirt near the bridge, one facing death, then barred inside the fortress.

In this remarkable verse, Nostradamus predicted very accurately the fate of Charles I. After the defeat and capture of Charles I in December 1648, he was imprisoned in Windsor Castle, which had 'fallen' to the Parliamentary forces led by Oliver Cromwell. From that moment on Charles was 'one facing death', as the outcome of his trial was never in doubt. On 30 January 1649, he was led to the Banqueting House in Whitehall, the place of his execution, wearing only a white shirt and no coat, and was beheaded. The blood-spattered shirt was displayed on a pole on London Bridge to the fear and horror of those who supported the monarchy.

[*Century 8, quatrain 37*]

1649

Grand & Bruceles marcheront contre Anvers.
Senat de Londres mettront à mort leur Roy.
Le sel & vin luy seront à l'envers,
Pour aux avoir le regne en desarroy.

Ghent and Brussels will march against Antwerp. The Senate of London will put their king to death. The salt and wine will be the wrong way round for him, for them to have the kingdom in disarray.

This quatrain undeniably refers to the execution of Charles I in 1649. The first part reflects the machinations in Europe, with Philip IV trying to reconquer the Netherlands but eventually giving the Dutch control of several towns, which ultimately ruined Antwerp. The second line clearly refers to the execution, although the latter part of the quatrain is more obscure.

[*Century 9, quatrain 49*]

1649 and 1655

Le juste à tort à mort l'on viendra mettre
Publiquement, & du milieu estaint;
Si grande peste en ce lieu viendra naistre,
Que les jugeans fouyr seront contraints.

They shall come to put the just man wrongfully to death publicly and in the midst of a crowd he is extinguished. So great a plague shall come to be born in this place that the judges shall be forced to run away.

In this verse, Nostradamus is referring to the execution of Charles I, the 'just man wrongfully' and publicly put to death. Nostradamus was a committed royalist and believed in the divine right of the monarchy to rule, and would have regarded the killing of a king with horror. In this quatrain, he implies that the Great Plague, which killed thousands of people in London sixteen years later, may have been some form of divine retribution meted out to the perpetrators of the crime.

[*Century 9, quatrain 11*]

1650

La bande foible le terre occupera
Ceux du haut lieu feront horribles cris.
Le gros troupeau d'estre coin troublera,
Tombe pres D. nebro descouvers les escris.

The band who are weak will occupy the land, horrible cries will be made by those in high places. The great herd of the troubled, outer corner, very near Edinburgh, falls by the writings discovered.

This has been interpreted as referring to the Battle of Dunbar, fought twenty-five miles east of Edinburgh in 1650. Cromwell's forces were outnumbered by the Scots who were nevertheless victorious. Cromwell subsequently took possession of important documents which may explain the reference in the last line.

[*Century 8, quatrain 56*]

1651 or 1940s

Sur la minuict conducteur de l'armée
Se sauvera subit esvanovy,
Sept ans apres la fame non blasmée,
A son retour ne dira oncq ouy.

At midnight the leader of the army will save himself, disappearing suddenly. Seven years after, his fame not blamed, at his return he will not say yes.

This is a rather general quatrain that can be applied to two events, one in 1651 and the other in the 1940s. In 1651, Charles II fled after his defeat at the Battle of Worcester. Cromwell then took power for seven years after the military coup of 1653. After Cromwell died in 1658, his son tried to maintain the lord protectorship but abdicated in 1659. Charles II was returned to the throne in 1660, with the help of the army.

An alternative interpretation involves General MacArthur who in 1942 withdrew from the Philippines, returning in 1944 when he successfully captured them. Seven years later, he lost his command. The reference to 'yes' could be a vague connection to his presidential hopes—about which he never did confirm his intentions.

[*Century 10, quatrain 4*]

1655

Classe Gauloise n'approches de Corsegne,
Moins de Sardaigne tu t'en repentiras,
Trestous mourrez frustrez de l'aide grogne.
Sang nagera captif ne me croiras.

French fleet, do not approach Corsica, even less Sardinia, you will repent of it. You will all die, frustrated of aid from the cape, captive, swimming in blood, you shall not believe me.

This quatrain is believed to refer to an incident involving the French fleet when it was passing through the Gulf of Lyons in 1655, near Corsica and Sardinia. Several vessels sank in rough seas and many drowned, being unable to reach the nearest land, the Cape de Porceau (in the original French, the word for 'cape' is *grogne*, which can also mean a pig's snout).

[*Century 3, quatrain 87*]

---

c.1660

A temps du dueil que le felin monarque,
Guerroyera le jeune Aemathien.
Gaule bransler, perecliter la barque,
Tenter Phossens au ponant entretien.

In the time of mourning, when the feline monarch shall make war against the young Aemathien. France shall quake, the ship (or bark) being in danger, Phocens shall be tempted, a talk in the west.

This quatrain is full of interpretive translations without which it is of little significance. The time of mourning could refer to that of Louis XIII because Aemathien ('the child of the dawn') seems to indicate Louis XIV, the Sun King. The feline monarch would then be Philip IV of Spain, who pursued the war against Louis. Phocens is almost certainly Marseilles, which was founded by the Phoceans. The 'talk in the west' may refer to when Louis went to the west of France to conclude the Peace of the Pyrenees. At the end of Louis XIV's reign, France was the leading power in Europe.

[*Century 10, quatrain 58*]

1665

La grande peste de cité maritime
Ne cessera que mort ne soit vengee;
Du juste sang par pris damne sans crime,
De la grand' dame par fainte n'outragee.

The great plague in the maritime city will not cease until the death is avenged of the just blood by price condemned for no crime; the great lady is outraged by the feigning.

In this quatrain, Nostradamus predicts the Great Plague of London ('the maritime city'), which he believes will afflict the people as a result of the execution of Charles I. (Charles I is 'the just blood by price condemned for no crime'.) In this prophecy, 'the great lady' represents the Catholic Church, 'outraged' by the rising tide of Protestantism, which was soon to be established as the form of religion in England. Nostradamus was a devout Catholic and his disapproval of Protestantism can be found in many of his writings.

[*Century 2, quatrain 53*]

1666

Le sang du iuste à Londres sera faute,
Bruslez par foudres de vingt trois les six,
La dame antique cherra de place haute,
De mesme secte plusieurs seront occis.

The blood of the just shall be demanded of London, burnt by fire in three times twenty and six. The ancient lady shall fall from her high place, and many of the same sect shall be killed.

In this remarkable quatrain, Nostradamus accurately predicts and gives a date for the Great Fire of London in 1666. The 'ancient lady' may be St Paul's Cathedral, more specifically, a statue of the Virgin Mary from the steeple. 'Many of the same sect' refers to both the churches (eighty-seven of which were destroyed) and their congregations. The fire claimed the lives of many Londoners, and the 'blood of the just' underlines the fact that they were innocent victims of this tragedy.

[*Century 2, quatrain 51*]

1685

Seicher de faim, de soif gent Genevoise,
Espoir prochain viendra au defaillir,
Sur point tremblant sera loy Gebenoise,
Classe au grand port ne se peut accueillir.

The people of Geneva shall be dried up with hunger and thirst, an imminent hope shall come to fainting: The law of the Cévennes will be at a trembling point, the fleet cannot be received at the great port.

In 1685, Louis XIV revoked the Edict of Nantes (1584), which forced Protestants in France to choose either conversion to the Catholic faith or exclusion from the nation. Louis was determined to drive the heretics out of France. The move caused uproar amongst Protestants and rebellion in some cities. The ships referred to must have been carrying supplies across Lake Geneva to the people who were under siege.

[*Century 2, quatrain 64*]

Le nay difforme par horreur suffoqué,
Dans la cité du grand Roy habitable,
L'edit severe des captifs revoque,
Gresle & tonnerre Condon inestimable.

One born deformed, by horror suffocated, in the city inhabited by the great king. The severe edict of the captives shall be revoked, hail and thunder, Condon inestimable.

In the first part of the quatrain, Nostradamus may be describing the so-called 'man in the iron mask', who was alleged to be the illegitimate son of Louis XIV's queen, Maria Theresa, and Cardinal Mazarin. The 'severe edict revoked' may be the Edict of Nantes, which was dissolved by Louis XIV. Nostradamus disliked this edict because it gave freedom of worship to Protestants so he may well have described it in these terms.

[*Century 5, quatrain 97*]

1687–1690

Le Roy Gaulois par la Celtique dextre,
Voyant discorde de la grand Monarchie,
Sur les trois parts fera fleurir son sceptre,
Contre la cappe de la grand Hierarchie.

The Gallic king by the Celtic right hand, viewing the discord of the great monarch, will flourish his sceptre over the three leopards against the French king of the great hierarchy.

This quatrain once again appears to elaborate on the theme of the two preceding ones. The opening line refers to William of Orange, Stadholder of Holland, who sees the problems that James II is experiencing and takes over the throne of Britain. The three leopards are Nostradamus' way of describing the royal lions of English heraldry. It was a more or less bloodless takeover as William had many supporters in Britain and was married to James' daughter, Mary. France was alarmed at the course of events and supported James in his efforts to regain the throne.

[*Century 2, quatrain 69*]

1688

Trente de Londres secret conjureront,
Contre leur Roy sur le pont l'entreprinse,
Luy, satalites la mort degousteront.
Un Roy esleu blonde, natif de Frize.

Thirty of London shall secretly conspire against their king, the enterprise made upon the sea. He and his adherents shall be put off by death. A blond-haired king, native of Friesland.

This verse describes the machinations that surrounded the deposition of the last Stuart king, James II, and the succession to the throne of William of Orange (William III) and Queen Mary. The king in the first line is the Catholic James II, who succeeded to the throne in 1685 amid considerable hostility. This reached new heights when a son and heir was born in 1688 and was baptised into the Catholic faith. Thirty Protestant noblemen conspired secretly and signed a document that was taken by Admiral Herbert to Friesland (the Netherlands) to the stadholder, William of Orange, and his wife Mary, the daughter of James II. The petition requested that the Protestant William should sail to England and oust his father-in-law, and pledged that the signatories would give him their support. William was an heir in his own right, being the grandson of Charles I, and he sailed to England, landing on 5 November 1688. A few weeks later James and his followers, fearful of the prospect of death, escaped to exile in France. The colour of William's hair is not known, but he was certainly from Friesland.

[*Century 4, quatrain 89*]

1688–1689

La blonde au nez forché viendra commettre
Par le duelle & chassera dehors,
Les exilez dedans fera remettre
Aux lieux marins commettant les plus forts.

The blond one shall do battle with the forked nose and chase him out in a duel. He will have put back the exiles, committing the strongest of them to the marine places.

William of Orange is the 'blond one' referred to in this quatrain and his faction drove out his father-in-law, James II (the 'forked nose'), in 1688. James and his Stuart followers ('the exiles') withdrew to Ireland and, with the aid of the French navy, engaged in sea battles against British forces. They had some notable successes, particularly off Beachy Head, but defeat at the Battle of the Boyne in Ireland itself proved decisive and James was forced to retreat to France.

[*Century 2, quatrain 67*]

De l'Aquilon les efforts seront grands,
Sur l'Ocean sera la porte ouverte,
Le regne en l'isle sera reintegrand,
Tremblera Londres par voille descouverte.

The efforts of the north shall be great, across the ocean the gate shall be open. The reign on the island shall be re-established, London shall tremble when the sails are sighted.

This continues the theme of quatrain 67, the 'efforts of the north' being those of William of Orange. The indecisive British naval commander, the Earl of Torrington, was responsible for losing several battles. The 'gate' of the sea was left open for a strong naval force to take the British Isles. The 'reign on the island' refers to James's time in Ireland, and London 'trembling' probably reflects the insecurity of people in England.

[*Century 2, quatrain 68*]

1701–1713

Par mort la France prendra voyage à faire,
Classe par mer, marcher monts Pyrenees,
Espagne en trouble, marcher gent militaire,
Des plus grand dames en France emmenees.

Due to a death France shall undertake a journey, the fleet at sea, they shall march across the Pyrenean mountains. Spain in trouble, an army on the march. Some of the greatest ladies shall be taken into France.

This quatrain is usually taken to describe the wars that followed the succession to the Spanish throne in 1700 of Philip V, the heir of Charles II of Spain. As Philip's grandfather was Louis XIV of France, his succession caused alarm among a group of countries, which formed a coalition against him. These countries included Britain, Holland, Austria and Prussia, who rallied in support of another pretender to the throne, Archduke Charles. France launched her navy and the French army marched over the Pyrenees. The war in Spain lasted for twelve years. The 'greatest ladies' referred to in the last line are probably the Spanish princesses who married Louis XIII and Louis XIV respectively and produced the royal heirs to the throne.

[*Century 4, quatrain 2*]

1714

Croix paix soubs un, accomply divin verbe,
Espaigne & Gaule seront unis ensemble,
Grand clade proche, & combat tresacerbe,
Cœur si hardy ne sera qui ne tremble.

Cross, peace, under one accomplished the divine word. Spain and France will be united together. A great disaster is near at hand, the fighting very sharp, no heart so brave that shall not tremble.

This quatrain may allude to the brief period during which France and Spain were united, when Philip V became heir to the Spanish throne in 1700. Philip was the grandson of Louis XIV of France and heir of Charles II of Spain. The 'disaster' that is 'near at hand' is the War of the Spanish Succession, which lasted until 1713. The reference to the 'cross, peace, under one accomplished the divine word' may allude to a papal bull, entitled *Unigenitus*, which was issued by the Pope in 1713.

[*Century 4, quatrain 5*]

1714

Apres viendra des extremes contrees
Prince Germain sur le throsne doré.
En servitude & par eaux rencontrees
La dame serve son temps plus n'adoré.

After that there will come out of distant lands, a German prince upon the golden throne. The servitude encountered from over the waters, the lady so served in the times no more adored.

This prophecy has been attributed to the accession of the Hanoverian prince, George I, to the English crown ('the golden throne') in 1714. Germany was regarded as a remote country in Nostradamus' day, and George I was Queen Anne's cousin. (German in the original French may mean German but also 'relative'.) 'Servitude' for England came by design rather than conquest, as George I was asked to accept the prestigious 'golden throne' of England. The 'lady' is assumed to be the Roman Catholic Church, which declined under the Hanoverians, but may mean Queen Anne.

[*Century 2, quatrain 87*]

1729–1796

Vers Aquilon grands efforts par hommasse
Presque l'Europe & l'univers vexer,
Les deux eclypses mettra en telle chasse,
Et aux Pannons vie & mort renforcer.

Towards the north great efforts by a masculine woman, trouble Europe and almost all the universe. The two eclipses shall be put into such a flight that they will reinforce life and death for the Poles.

This may describe Catherine the Great, Empress of Russia, who succeeded in winning the affection and loyalty of her subjects even although she came to the country as a foreign princess. Catherine was German-born and had received a fine French education. She was regarded at the time as an enlightened leader who corresponded with learned writers and philosophers, such as Voltaire, Diderot and other French Encyclopedists. Catherine attempted to improve the lives of the Russian serfs and to bring about other reforms in the earlier years of her reign, but with limited success. However, her ideas were considered to be so dangerous that her writings, the *Instructions*, were banned in France. In the end, the French Revolution and the fear that this aroused among all the royal and aristocratic houses curtailed any further reforms. Catherine was astute in foreign policy and gained territory for Russia. This was at no time more apparent than in the series of partitions of Poland, that began in 1772 and lasted until that land was eventually brought under Russian control in 1775.

[*Century 8, quatrain 15*]

1737

Le successeur de la Duché viendra,
Beaucoup plus outre que la mer de Toscane,
Gauloise branche la Florence tiendra,
Dans son giron d'accord nautique Rane.

The successor to the Duchy shall come from far beyond the sea of Tuscany. A French branch shall hold Florence, in its wake a nautical agreement concerning the frog.

Florence was the capital city of the dukedom of Tuscany, and in 1737 passed for the first time to the powerful French family of the Duke of Lorraine. The 'Duchy' stayed with the Lorraine family until 1859, except during the turbulent years of the French Revolution.

[*Century 5, quatrain 3*]

1745–1746

Sous le terroir du rond globe lunaire,
Lors que sera dominateur Mercure,
L'isle d'Escosse sera un luminaire,
Qui les Anglois mettra à deconfiture.

Under the territory of the round lunar globe, at a time when Mercury shall be dominant, the island of Scotland shall produce a luminary, who shall put the English at discomfort.

This verse would seem appropriately to describe Prince Charles Edward Stuart, the Young Pretender, and his Jacobite followers who put the English into discomfort as far south as Derby. It has been the subject of much speculation as to what might have been the eventual outcome had Prince Charles Edward Stuart and his followers continued their march to London.

[*Century 5, quatrain 93*]

1754–1793

Le trop bon temps, trop de bonté royale,
Faicts & deffaicts prompt, subit, negligence.
Leger croira faux d'espouse loyale,
Luy mis à mort par sa benevolence.

An excess of good times and too much royal bounty, made and promptly unmade by sudden negligence. He will lightly believe his loyal spouse to be false, and will cause her death through his benevolence.

Louis XVI made many disastrous mistakes in the early years of his reign which directly fostered the events that led up to the French Revolution. He readily listened to false reports about his wife, Marie Antoinette, who was foolish and extravagant rather than disloyal. And in the end, the accumulation of errors led them both to death by execution in 1793.

[*Century 10, quatrain 43*]

1769

Un Empereur naistra pres d'Italie,
Qui à l'Empire sera vendu bien cher,
Diront avec quels gens il se ralie
Qu'on trouvera moins Prince que boucher.

An Emperor will be born near to Italy, who will cost the Empire very dear. They will say, with what people he keeps company. One will find him less a prince than a butcher.

This quatrain is universally taken to refer to the birth of Napoleon I. He was born in Corsica, which until two years previously had belonged to Italy. However, it was bought by France (by Louis XV), hence the birthplace being 'near to Italy'. The 'people' with whom he kept company could have several interpretations, including the parentage of his wife, Josephine, or his brothers, who were given exalted positions in other states. There is certainly no doubt that he cost his country very dear indeed. Vast numbers of men died in the various military campaigns, and many of the territorial gains were subsequently lost. The country was much weaker after his rule was ended than when he came to power.

[*Century 1, quatrain 60*]

D'un nom farouche tel proferé sera,
Que les trois sœurs auront fato le nom.
Puis peuple grand par langue & fait dira,
Plus que nul autre aura bruit & renom.

By a wild name one will be called, that three sisters will have from fate. Then a great people by words and deeds shall say, he shall have fame and renown more than anyone else.

This quatrain is rather more obscure than many and necessitates careful interpretation. It is, however, generally taken to refer to the birth of Napoleon I in 1769. The reference to 'fame and renown' is obvious, and he was well known for his great battle speeches to the troops before a conflict. However, the other factor that points to Napoleon, although in a somewhat convoluted way, is the use of the phrase 'wild name'. It is explained that the name Napoleon came from the Greek, meaning 'new exterminator', thus the link with 'wild (or 'barbaric') name'. There is a very subtle play on words which has to be sought. Taken at face value, the quatrain points to the coming of a messiah figure.

[*Century 1, quatrain 76*]

Napoleon or Hitler

Tasche de murdre, enormes adulteres,
Grand ennemy de tout le genre humain,
Que sera pire qu'ayeuls, oncles, ne peres,
En fer, feu, sanguin & inhumain.

Touched by murder and enormous adulteries, great enemy of all humanity, he will be worse than his forebears, uncles or fathers, in iron, fire, bloody and inhuman.

Napoleon was actually called this ('great enemy of all humanity') in his own lifetime by Morenigo, ambassador to Venice, but the quatrain is equally applicable to Hitler.

[*Century 10, quatrain 10*]

1783–1794

Istra du mont Gaulsier & Aventin,
Qui par le trou advertira l'armee;
Entre deux rocs sera prins le butin,
De Sext. mansol faillir la renommee.

Issued from Montgaulfier and the Aventine, one who through a hole shall alert the army. Between two rocks the booty shall be taken. The renown of Sextus, the one alone, shall fail.

This quatrain refers to the invention in 1783 of the hot air balloon by the Montgolfier brothers, Joseph Michel and Jacques Etienne, and its subsequent use for military reconnaissance (via a hole cut in the bottom of the basket). The balloon was used in this way at the Battle of Fleurus on 26 June 1794 in which the French won a resounding victory. Later they captured and looted Rome and the Aventine. 'Sextus, the one alone', is Pope Pius VI, who was driven out of Rome by Napoleon Bonaparte and died in exile. In 1797, he was forced to give up much of the Vatican land under the Treaty of Tolentino. This is the 'booty' taken 'between two rocks'.

[*Century 5, quatrain 57*]

1785–1794

Le tiers premier pis que ne fit Neron,
Vuidez vaillant que sang humain respandre
R'édifier fera le forneron,
Siècle d'or, mort, nouveau Roy grand esclandre.

The third first commits worse acts than Nero, go flow, brave human blood. The furnace, shall be rebuilt, a golden century, then death, a new king and awful scenes.

In this quatrain, Nostradamus refers to events leading up to the French Revolution. The 'golden century' was the reign of Louis XIV in particular (but also that of Louis XV)— gone forever. Following on from this was the crowning of the 'new king', Louis XVI, and then the terrible events of the Revolution, with the deaths of the royal family and many other citizens, and 'brave human blood' flowing from the guillotine ('awful scenes'). The guillotine was put up in the Place de la Révolution opposite the Palace of the Tuileries, where there had previously been situated the kilns of a tile 'factory'. The guillotine was the new 'furnace', responsible for so much terror in Revolutionary France. 'The third first' refers to the National Assembly, set up by the Third Estate (the Commons), one of several bodies set up during the years of Revolution. Certainly during this period, acts of cruelty equalling and surpassing those of the Emperor Nero were committed in France.

[*Century 9, quatrain 17*]

1789

Quand la lictiere du tourbillon versee
Et seront faces de leurs manteaux couverts,
La republique par gens nouueaux vexee,
Lors blancs & rouges jugeront à l'envers.

When the litter is turned over by the wind and faces are hidden by cloaks, the republic be will troubled by new people and both the whites and the reds will rule wrongly.

This would seem to be a clear anticipation of revolution and in particular the French Revolution. The 'litter' was a common mode of transport for members of the aristocracy, and their being 'turned over by the wind' alludes to the turbulence of revolution and to the overthrow of the monarchy.

Faces 'hidden by cloaks' could have at least two interpretations. It might be conjuring an image of members of that same aristocracy who fled from the country, probably in disguise, and certainly in as covered a fashion as possible. It may, however, have a more gruesome meaning—it could represent the heads of those executed on the guillotine, which literally fell out of sight.

It is unusual to find a reference to the 'republic', something with which people would not have been familiar at the time the Prophecies were made known. The 'new people' are the revolutionaries and the significance of 'the whites' and 'reds' is readily understood. A white cockade was the emblem of the Bourbon kings, while the revolutionaries used red as their colour.

Interestingly, there is another revolution that to some extent fits this quatrain—the Russian Revolution of 1917. The Red and White Russians fit the essence of the last line admirably.

[*Century 1, quatrain 3*]

> *De gens esclave, chansons, chants & requestes,*
> *Captifs par Princes & Seigneur aux prisons.*
> *A l'advenir par idiots sans testes,*
> *Seront receus par divins oraisons.*

From enslaved peoples, held captive by princes and lords, come songs, chants and requests. In the future, these will be received by idiots without heads as divine oratory.

This seems to point clearly, once again, to the French Revolution, and there are a number of identifiable features. The songs and chants are those of the mob, seeking freedom from their enslavement. The 'idiots without heads' are literally those victims of Madame La Guillotine (both the Revolutionary ringleaders, in addition to the aristocracy before them) and metaphorically those with little or no political wisdom. Were it not for the allusion to the guillotine, this could be a further reference to the Russian Revolution of 1917, particularly as an alternative use of the word 'enslaved' could refer to a Slav people.

[*Century 1, quatrain 14*]

> *Avant long temps le tout sera rangé.*
> *Nous esperons vn siecle bien senestre.*
> *L'estat des masques & des seule bien changé,*
> *Peu trouveront qu'à son rang vueillent estre.*

1789

Before long all things shall be arranged. We look for a very evil century. The state of the masks and those alone very much changed, few will discover that they wish to keep their rank.

This quatrain refers to the turbulent times of the French Revolution, when it was dangerous to be a member of the aristocracy or court ('masks') or a priest ('those alone'). People belonging to these social groups found their status very much altered and risked death and financial ruin. Priests were abolished in 1790 but later restored.

[*Century 2, quatrain 10*]

Le regne prins le Roy conviera,
La dame prinse a mort jurez a sort,
La vie a Royne fils on desniera,
Et la pillex au forte de la consort.

The kingdom taken, the King will invite, the lady taken to her death, sworn by lot. They will deny the life to the Queen's son and the mistress to the lot of the wife.

There are a number of differences in the original words of this quatrain, depending upon the source. However, it is generally agreed that this refers to a number of events during the French Revolution. Following the storming of the Bastille, Louis XVI was left helpless to deal with the popular unrest, and many aristocrats were fleeing France. In June 1791, Louis and his family tried to escape but were captured and imprisoned. The National Assembly kept the king as a figurehead until the new constitution had been established and the new Legislative Assembly was in place. In 1792, amid war with Austria that initially went badly, the people demanded a republic. Louis was executed on 21 January 1793, in the early days of the new republic. It seems that the last part of the quatrain refers to the fact that the queen and Louis' mistress, Marie Antoinette and Madame du Barry respectively, suffered a similar fate, and indeed both were imprisoned. The queen was eventually executed in October 1793. The reference to 'sworn by lot' is interesting because the queen was tried by a tribunal that comprised a jury with members chosen by lot, something unknown to Nostradamus.

[*Century 9, quatrain 77*]

1789–1793

D'esprit de regne munisememens descriees,
Et seront peuples esmeus contre leur Roy,
Paix, fait nouveau, sainctes loix empirees,
Paris onc fut en si tresdur arroy.

The spirit of the kingdom shall denounce municipal rule and the people shall rise up against their king. A new peace is made, holy laws made worse, Paris was never in such great disarray.

A quatrain that depicts the general state of discontent and disorder during the days of the French Revolution in Paris. Old laws and traditions were turned upside down, the king was executed in 1793, and for a time the capital was in a state close to anarchy.

[*Century 6, quatrain 23*]

1789–1810

Grand Po, grand mal pour Gaulois recevra,
Vaine terreur au maritin Lyon;
Peuple infiny par la mer passera,
Sans eschapper un quart d'un million.

Great Po will receive great harm from the Frenchman, vain terror to the maritime lion. Infinite people will pass across the sea, a quarter of a million shall not escape.

Once again this quatrain refers to the Napoleonic Wars, particularly the sufferings of Italy (the 'Great Po'). Allusion is made to British fears about Napoleon ('the maritime lion') although these proved to be groundless since no invasion took place. In 1798, Napoleon took his armies across the sea into Egypt and during the ensuing conflict, many thousands of lives were lost.

[*Century 2, quatrain 94*]

1790

Las qu'on verra grand peuple tourmenté,
Et la Loy saincte en totale ruyne,
Par autres loix toute la Chrestienté,
Quand d'or, d'argent trouve nouvelle mine.

Alas, how a great people will be tormented and the holy law in total ruin. By other laws, all Christianity, when new mines of gold, and of silver will find.

This quatrain fits quite nicely with the disestablishment of the clergy in France and its subsequent persecution. The 'other laws' would be the Cult of Reason (*see also* 1793, page 97). The reference to gold and silver could then be the possessions that were taken from the clergy.

[*Century 1, quatrain 53*]

Yeus clos ouverts d'antique fantasie
L'habit des seules seront mis à néant;
Le grand monarque chastira leur frenaisie
Ravir des temples le thresor par devant.

1790–1814

Eyes shut shall be opened by an ancient fantasy, the habit of those alone shall be brought to nothing. The great monarch shall punish their frenzy, ravishing the treasure in front of the temples.

This quatrain refers to the suppression of the Catholic Church during the French Revolution. The wearing of religious garments was prohibited in 1789, before the priests themselves were abolished in 1790. The people's 'eyes' were closed to the Christian faith. Both Louis XVI and Napoleon ('the great monarch') robbed and suppressed the monasteries. Napoleon was later forced to restore the Catholic faith and seek help from the Pope.

[*Century 2, quatrain 12*]

1790–1814

Foudre en Bourgogne fera cas portenteux,
Que par engin homme ne pourroit faire,
De leur senat sacrifiste fait boyteux,
Fera sçavoir aux ennemis l'affaire.

Lightning in Burgundy with portentous events, that which could never have been done by trickery. The lame priest will make affairs of their senate known to the enemies.

This quatrain describes Charles Maurice de Tallyrand-Périgord, a lame priest who rose to a position of prominence during the French Revolution and in the period when the country was led by Napoleon. Tallyrand held the position of Grand Chamberlain but became increasingly dissatisfied with Napoleon's policies, so much so that he resigned in 1807. After this time he was actively but covertly engaged in undermining the position of the emperor by secretly colluding with Tsar Alexander I of Russia.

Tallyrand was instrumental in convening the senate in April 1814 which decreed that Napoleon must relinquish the crown.

[*Century 2, quatrain 76*]

1791

De nuict viendra par la forest de Reines,
Deux pars voltorte Herne, la pierre blanche,
Le moine noir en gris dedans Varennes,
Esleu cap. cause tempeste, feu, sang tranche.

By night shall come through the forest of Reins two by a roundabout way; the Queen, the white stone, the monk king dressed in grey, within Varennes the elected Capet causes tempest, fire, bloody slicing.

In this quatrain, Nostradamus predicts the flight of Louis XVI and Marie Antoinette from the Palace of the Tuileries through the Forest of Reins. They were attempting to escape from France but were captured at Varennes. The king was said to have been disguised as a monk dressed in a grey cloak, and the queen usually wore a white gown. It was also alleged that the queen's hair turned suddenly white after their capture, when she realized the peril that faced the royal family. These factors may explain the reference to the 'white stone'. The earlier intransigence of the king and his refusal to listen to the legitimate grievances of his people certainly helped to cause the bloody events of the Revolution and sealed his own fate and that of his family.

[*Century 9, quatrain 20*]

Le grand Chyren soy saisir d'Avignom,
De Rome lettres en miel plein d'amertume
Lettre ambassade partir de Chanignon,
Carpentras pris par duc noir rouge plume.

The great Henry will seize Avignon, from Rome letters in honey, full of bitterness. Lettera and ambassadors shall go from Chanignon, Carpentras taken by the black duke with a red feather.

Avignon was at one time the seat of papal power, and Nostradamus is here referring to its seizure by the French king. 'Chanignon' is unrecognized, but Carpentras is near Avignon and was also under the rule of the Vatican. The superficially sweet letters that actually were very bitter presumably came from the Vatican. This event did not happen until 1791, thus the reference to Henry is not accurate except to represent French royalty. Also, the actual word in the quatrain is 'Chyren', which is almost an anagram for Henry but may have another significance.

[*Century 9, quatrain 41*]

1791–1793

Trois cens seront d'un vouloir & accord,
Que pour venir au bout de leur attainte.
Vingt mois apres tous & records,
Leur Roy trahir simulant haine fainte.

Three hundred shall be of one mind and agreement that they may come to attain their end; twenty months after, by all of them and their deliberations, their king will be betrayed simulating a feigned hatred.

This quatrain appears to allude to the trial and eventual execution of King Louis XVI. Louis and the royal family were intercepted in June 1791 while attempting to flee from France.

The National Assembly used the king as a figurehead, forcing him to sign legislative papers, particularly the new constitution that came into effect in September of that year. The National Assembly then dissolved itself, and a new body was formed called the Legislative Assembly. By July of 1792 the French people were demanding that the king should be thrown out and a republic declared. The Assembly finally decided that the king should stand trial and this took place in December 1792. He was executed on 21 January 1793.

[*Century 5, quatrain 37*]

1791–1793 and 1851

Esleu sera Renad ne sonnant mot,
Faisant le saint public vivant pain d'orge,
Tyrannizer apres tant à un cop,
Mettant à pied des plus grands sur la gorge.

A fox shall be elected without sounding one word, feigning saintliness in public, living on barley bread. Afterwards he shall suddenly become a tyrant, placing his foot upon the throat of the greatest ones.

This quatrain aptly describes the life and career of Maximilien Robespierre during the French Revolution. Robespierre became prominent in 1791 when, as a lawyer, he became public prosecutor for the Criminal Tribunal of the Seine. He was in sympathy with the ideas of the Jacobins, an extreme wing of the Republican movement, and soon became their leader. In 1792, he was elected as a member of the National Convention and soon became its dominant force. He was vehement in his role as prosecutor in the trial of Louis XVI and in his demands for the king's execution. Following this event in January 1793,

Robespierre was a leading figure in the establishment of the Revolutionary Tribunal, Committee of Public Safety and Reign of Terror. Georges Jacques Danton, a lawyer and leader of the right-wing Republican movement, the Girondins, who had aided Robespierre, was soon elbowed aside. By 1793, Robespierre (nicknamed 'fox') was a virtual dictator, and all French citizens lived in fear of the guillotine. He adopted an austere lifestyle, but his reign of tyranny, although brief, became notorious for its bloodthirsty nature. Eventually, in 1794, both Robespierre and Danton were themselves sent to the guillotine to which they had consigned so many others.

[*Century 8, quatrain 41*]

1792

Sous ombre saincte d'oster de servitude,
Peuple & cité l'usurpera luy-mesmes,
Pire fera par faux de jeune pute,
Livré au champ lisant le faux poesme.

Beneath the feigned shadow of removing servitude, the people and the city shall themselves usurp power. He shall do worse because of the fraudulence of a young whore, betrayed in the field reading a false poem.

Nostradamus seems to be writing here about the French Revolution, Louis XVI and Marie Antoinette. The Revolution falsely proclaimed greater freedom for the common people, but the reality was far from being the case. Marie Antoinette is described in scathing terms in this quatrain. She was indeed hated for her extravagance at a time when ordinary people were almost starving, and she was also suspected of having an adulterous affair with a cardinal. In 1792 the royal family were placed in the Temple, and the king promised not to attempt an escape.

However, this promise was broken and the family were intercepted and captured at Varennes in June 1792.

[*Century 5, quatrain 5*]

La grand pitié sera sans long tarder,
Ceux qui dônoient seront contraints de prendre,
Nuds affamez de froid, soif, soy bander,
Passer les monts en faisant grand esclandre.

The great pity shall happen before too long. Those that gave shall be constrained to take. Naked, famished with cold, thirsty, they shall band together to pass over the mountains causing a great scandal.

In 1792, France declared the disestablishment of the Church and announced the Cult of Reason. Many priests found themselves prosecuted and without support, and, having previously given alms themselves, now were forced to take whatever they could obtain in order to survive. Many priests left France altogether, crossing the Alps and hoping to make a fresh start elsewhere in Europe. Their plight was the subject of great concern among Christian people.

[*Century 6, quatrain 69*]

La part solus mary sera mitré,
Retour conflict passera sur la thuille.
Par cinq cens un trahyr sera tiltré,
Narbon & Saulce par coutaux avons d'huille.

The married partner, solitary, shall wear a mitre, returning, conflict, he shall pass over the tiles. By five hundred one traitor shall be dignified; Narbonne and Saulce shall have oil for knives.

This quatrain has been closely analysed by many commentators who have been struck by the wealth of detail about events that took place so long after the death of Nostradamus. When Louis XVI and Marie Antoinette fled from the Palace of the Tuileries in 1791, they spent the following night at the house of the Saulce family in Varennes. Saulce was mayor of the city and also a chandler who sold oil. Nostradamus seems to imply that Saulce was a traitor who betrayed the king and queen and received some recognition for this act. Reference is also made in the verse to Narbonne, who was the Minister for War. The 'solitary, married partner' who 'shall wear a mitre' was the king himself, who returned 'over the tiles' to the Tuileries Palace in June 1792. A mob of exactly five hundred citizens (according to accounts at the time) invaded the palace, arrested the king and made him put on a revolutionary cap of liberty, which looked like a mitre. In Nostradamus' time, the Palace of the Tuileries did not exist but the site was occupied by kilns for making tiles, and this is referred to in another quatrain (*see* Century 9, quatrain 17, pages 84–85).

[*Century 9, quatrain 34*]

1792–1795

Avant venuë de ruyne Celtique,
Dedans le temple deux parlementeront.
Poignar cœur, d'un monté au coursier & pique
Sans faire bruit le grand enterreront.

Before the coming of the French ruin, within the temple two shall talk in parliament. Stabbed to the heart by one mounted on a charger and with a lance, without making noise they shall buy the great one.

This verse may concern the fate of the second son of Louis XVI and Marie Antoinette, Louis XVII. All the royal family were imprisoned in the Temple in 1792 when revolutionary fervour was at its height. The king was executed in January 1793, and his oldest son died in 1795. However, there was considerable uncertainty about the fate of Louis XVII, who was separated from the rest of his family and kept in dreadful conditions in a dark dungeon. Nostradamus appears to indicate that the boy was killed by an unknown assassin and buried secretly. The official version of events was that Louis became seriously ill in May 1795 and died on 8 June. He was said to have been buried in an unmarked grave in St Marguerite's Church on 10 June. It appears that this account was disbelieved by certain people at the time. Some thought Louis had escaped and others that he had been murdered, as suggested by Nostradamus. As with the Russian Grand Duchess Anastasia, a century later, speculation continued, and in the succeeding years, several men claimed to be the royal prince.

[*Century 5, quatrain 1*]

1793

En bref seront de retour sacrifices,
Contrevenans seront mis à martyre,
Plus ne seront Moines, Abbez, Novices.
Le miel sera beaucoup plus cher que cire.

In a brief time sacrifices will return. Those who are opposed will be made martyrs. There will be no more monks, abbots or novices. Honey will be far more expensive than (bees) wax.

At this time, the revolutionary government in France disestablished the Church and abolished the worship of God. This was called the Cult of Reason. The clergy was therefore also abolished, and those who refused to accept this new proclamation were persecuted ('made martyrs'). The last sentence alludes to

1793

the decline in the use of candles (beeswax), which rendered the wax cheaper than honey, whereas before the wax was very expensive as it was used for candles lit in the offering of vows.

[*Century 1, quatrain 44*]

> *Par grand discord la trombe tremblera,*
> *Accord rompu, dressant la teste au ciel,*
> *Bouche sanglante dans le sang nagera,*
> *Au sol sa face oingte de laict & miel.*

By great discord the trumpet will tremble. Agreement broken, lifting the head to the sky, the bloody mouth shall swim in blood, the face, anointed with milk and honey, to the sun.

The French Revolution features again here, and in particular the execution of Louis XVI. The 'great discord' clearly refers to the breakdown between monarchy and the National Assembly, and the blood reflects the execution itself. The head that then lay facing the sun had been anointed with milk and honey at the coronation.

[*Century 1, quatrain 57*]

> *Le charbon blanc du noir sera chassé,*
> *Prisonnier fait mené au tumbereau,*
> *Moré Chameau sur pieds entrelassez,*
> *Lors le puisné filera l'aubereau.*

The white coal shall be chased out by the black, made a prisoner led to a cart; his feet are lashed together like a camel when the youngest shall slip the falcon.

A complicated quatrain in which the reader has to decipher anagrams in order to attempt to understand the meaning. 'White coal' (*charbon blanc*) stands for the Bourbon royal line, the king being Louis XVI who was captured, imprisoned and condemned by revolutionary forces. He was bound and carried to the place of execution on a cart, like so many others in the subsequent years of Terror, and met his death on 27 January 1793. Nostradamus seems to hint that Louis's youngest son may have escaped. This was a subject of speculation, but the older surviving son and heir, Charles Louis, died in 1795.

[*Century 4, quatrain 85*]

> *Des principaux de cité rebelée*
> *Qui tiendront fort pour liberté r'avoir;*
> *Detrencher masses infelice meslée,*
> *Cris urlemens a Nante piteux voir.*

Of the principal citizens of the rebellious city who will try hard to recover their liberty; the men are cut up, unhappy confusion, cries, howlings at Nantes pitiful to see.

This quatrain describes the terrible punishment meted out to the citizens of Nantes in 1793 for daring to try and assert their independence during the French Revolution. The people formed a body called the Central Assembly of Resistance to Oppression in alliance with like-minded neighbours. It was seen as a counter-revolution and brutally suppressed. Many of the men were guillotined while women, children and clergy were stripped naked, bound together in pairs and drowned in the River Loire. These events were called the Noyades ('drownings').

[*Century 5, quatrain 33*]

> *Prince de beauté tant venuste,*
> *Au chef menée, le second faict trahy;*
> *La cité au glaive de poudre face aduste,*
> *Par trop grand meurtre le chef du Roy hay.*

The prince of such exquisite beauty shall be brought to the chief, the second fact betrayed. The city given to the sword, of a powder the face burned; by too great a murder the chief of the king hated.

1793

This quatrain seems aptly to describe the fate of Louis XVI of France, who was considered to be an exceptionally handsome man. Louis was captured with his family in 1791 while attempting to escape from revolutionary France. The king was held as a captive and ordered by the Assembly to sign any papers considered necessary, including the new constitution in September 1791. This may be 'the second fact betrayed', for later, the king was tried and sent to the guillotine on 27 January 1793 and so was never allowed to be a constitutional monarch. The head of the king was burned in quicklime. Many other people lost their lives at this time.

[*Century 6, quatrain 92*]

> *Mort conspirée viendra en plein effect,*
> *Charge donnée & voyage de mort.*
> *Esleu, creé, receu, par siens deffaict,*
> *Sang d'innocence devant soy par remort.*

A death conspired for shall come to have its full effect, the charge given and the voyage of death. Elected, created, received, by his own defeated, the blood of innocence before him by remorse.

This quatrain describes the conspiracy and intrigue, culminating in execution, that surrounded the final two years of the life of Louis XVI. Louis had earlier been accepted, crowned and received by his own French people. Later, they turned upon him and conspired against him, first forcing him to become a constitutional monarch and then, when he had fulfilled their purposes in signing constitutional papers, sending him to his death. Nostradamus, who believed in the absolute rights of the monarchy, feels that the 'blood of innocence' was shed and in the bloodthirstiness of the Revolution, people came to be filled with remorse.

[*Century 8, quatrain 87*]

1793–1810

Du nom qui oncques ne fut au Roy Gaulois,
Jamais ne fust un foudre si craintif,
Tremblant l'Italie l'Espagne & les Anglois,
De femme estrangers grandement attentif.

Of a name that was never held by a French king, there never was so fearful a thunderbolt. Italy, Spain and the English tremble, he will be greatly attentive to foreign women.

These lines once again describe Napoleon Bonaparte who, as emperor, had a name that was quite distinct from those of the French royal lines. Napoleon was greatly feared by all the surrounding nations, who managed to defeat him only by uniting together. He was fond of foreign women, first marrying the Créole Josephine de Beauharnais, then later Marie Louise of Austria, and his mistress being the Polish Marie Walewska.

[*Century 4, quatrain 54*]

1793–1814

De la cité marine & tributaire,
La teste raze prendra la satrapie;
Chasser sordide qui puis sera contraire,
Par quatorze ans tiendra la tyrannie.

Of the marine city and tributary, the shaven head shall take the government; he shall chase out the sordid one who opposes him. For fourteen years he shall hold the tyranny.

Napoleon Bonaparte, a young lieutenant of just twenty-four years of age, led a successful campaign to recapture the French naval town of Toulon. The town was at that time in the command of English forces under Arthur Wellesley (later Lord Wellington). Later, when Napoleon started his political career, he wore his hair cut very short and was given the affectionate nickname of 'the little crop-head' by his soldiers. Napoleon chastened the power of the Directoire ('the sordid one') and ruled as emperor until 1814.

[*Century 7, quatrain 13*]

1794

Coq, chiens, & chats, de sang seront repeus,
Et de la playe du tyrant trouvé mort;
Au lict d'un autre jambes & bras rompus,
Qui n'avoit peu mourir de cruelle mort.

The cock, dogs and cats shall have had their fill of blood, when the tyrant is found dead of a wound in the bed of another, legs and arms broken; he who had no fear dies a cruel death.

The cock represents France, and the dogs and cats are the ordinary people who became sickened with the executions by guillotine during Maximilien Robespierre's Reign of Terror. Robespierre was arrested on 26 July 1794 but was soon freed by his troops of the commune, who escorted him to the Hôtel de Ville, where he spent the night ('bed of another'). The next day he was re-arrested by the National Guard and shot in the jaw during the affray. He did not, however, have his arms and legs broken. He and his allies suffered execution without trial the following day at the Place de la Révolution, where he had sent so many others to their deaths.

[*Century 2, quatrain 42*]

1795

Terre Italique pres des monts tremblera,
Lyon & Coq, non trop confederez,
En lieu de peur, l'un l'autre s'aidera,
Seul Castulon & Celtes moderez.

The Italian land near the mountains shall tremble. The lion and the cock shall not confer well together. In place of fear, each will help the other. Liberty alone moderates the French.

This quatrain refers to Napoleon's wars in Italy, which began in 1795, the mountains referred to being the Alps. Following the capture of Toulon and the commencement of the campaign, relationships between England ('the lion') and France ('the cock') became increasingly hostile. Later, under Louis XVIII, a spirit of cooperation was resumed, and the French were a nation free from the excesses of absolute monarchy.

[*Century 1, quatrain 93*]

Par le traffic du grand Lyon changé,
Et la plus-part tourné en pristine ruine,
Proye aux soldats par pille vendangé,
Par Iura mont & Sueue bruine.

The vast trade of great Lyons changed. The larger part turns into early ruin. A prey to soldiers by a harvest of pillage. In the mountains of Jura and Switzerland are fogs.

In October 1795, the city of Lyons was in a state of revolt against French revolutionary troops and had been besieged for two months. Many citizens lost their lives, and after troops entered the city, there was looting and damage on a considerable scale carried out by people who took advantage of the chaotic situation. However, there is no mention of mountain fogs in contemporary accounts.

[*Century 2, quatrain 83*]

> *L'armée Celtique contre les montagnars,*
> *Qui seront sceus & prins à la lipée;*
> *Paysans irez pouseront tost faugnars,*
> *Precipitez tous au fil de l'espée.*

The Celtic army shall go against the mountaineers who shall be revealed and caught in a trap. The angry peasants shall be pushed back into the marshes; they will all be put to the edge of the sword.

This verse may refer to a battle in Brittany between French Republican forces and Chouan peasants. The Chouans were defeated and most of them were killed, either during the battle or later when they were hunted down and executed.

[*Century 4, quatrain 63*]

> *En lieu du grand qui sera condamné,*
> *De prison hors son amy en sa place,*
> *L'espoir Troyen en six mois joint mort nay.*
> *Le Sol à l'urne seront prins fleuves en glace.*

In the place of the great one who shall be condemned, he is outside prison, his friend in his place. The Trojan hope in six months joined, stillborn; the sun in Aquarius, the rivers shall be frozen.

In this quatrain, Nostradamus may be adding to the controversy that surrounded the fate of Louis XVII, son and heir of Louis XVI, who was imprisoned during the Revolution along with the rest of his family but held separately from them. 'The Trojan hope' refers to the French royal line, and Nostradamus seems to imply that another child was substituted for the royal prince during the early months of 1795. It seems that this substitution, if indeed it took place, achieved very little but was 'stillborn', possibly meaning that both boys died. The official version of events, apparently supported by Nostradamus in Century 5, quatrain 1 (*see* pages 96–97), was that the young prince sickened and died on 8 June and was subsequently buried in an unmarked grave at the Church of St Marguerite on 10 June.

[*Century 6, quatrain 52*]

1796

A Cité neufue pensif pour condamner,
L'oysel de proye au ciel, se vient offrir,
Apres victoire à captifs pardonner,
Cremone & Mantoue grand maux aura à souffrir.

At the new city, thoughtful to condemn, the bird of prey offers himself to the sky. After victory, the captives shall be pardoned. At Cremona and Mantua much hardship will be suffered.

This quatrain can be related to Napoleon's Italian campaign. Without specific orders, Napoleon, having arrived at Villa Nova ('the new city'), then proceeded to Mantua. His army besieged the town, which held out for many months. When the town finally fell, Napoleon was generous to the inhabitants. Unfortunately, just two years later both Mantua and Cremona were occupied by the Austrians, who did not act so mercifully. The 'bird of prey' again refers to Napoleon himself.

[*Century 1, quatrain 24*]

Avant l'assaut oraison prononçee,
Milan prins d'Aigle par embusches deceus,
Muraille antique par canons enfoncee,
Par feu & sang à mercy peu receus.

1796

Before the assault an oration is pronounced, Milan is taken by the eagle being deceived by the ambush. The ancient walls are broken down by canons, in fire and blood few receive quarter.

This verse describes Napoleon's Italian campaign and, more specifically, the capture of Milan on 15 May 1796. Napoleon delivered to his poorly fed and ill-paid troops on the eve of the battle a rousing speech that fired them with enthusiasm. In fact, Milan surrendered without a fight, and it is likely that the last two lines refer to the ensuing battle for the city of Pavia. Here the citizens resisted the French attack, with the result that the city walls were destroyed by artillery bombardment and the town was sacked with great loss of life.

[*Century 3, quatrain 37*]

Pres du Tesin les habitans de Loyre,
Garonne & Saone, Seine, Tain, & Gironde,
Outre les monts dresseront promontoire,
Conflict donné, Pau granci, submergé onde.

Near the Tesin the inhabitants of the Loire, Garonne and Saonne, Seine, Tain and Gironde. Beside the mountains they will build a promontory, conflict given, Pau snatched, submerged by the wave.

Some commentators have suggested that 'Pau' is short for Napoleon in this quatrain. If this is correct, then this quatrain may relate to an incident during the Battle of Lodi. Apparently, during the fighting to capture the bridge over the River Adda, Napoleon plunged into the water and was saved from drowning by his men.

[*Century 6, quatrain 79*]

1797

Tout à l'entour de la grande cité,
Seront soldats logez par champs & villes,
Donner l'assaut Paris, Rome incité,
Sur le pont lors sera faite grand pille.

All surrounding the great city soldiers shall be billeted in fields and towns; Paris shall give the assault, Rome incited, on the bridge there will be great pillage.

This quatrain describes the sacking of Rome ('the great city') by French forces ('Paris') under the command of Napoleon Bonaparte in 1797 and 1808. Pope Pius VI was driven out of Rome and died in exile as a result of the first attack. Pope Pius VII was held captive on the occasion of the second assault in 1808. (*See also* 1808, pages 114–115.)

[*Century 5, quatrain 30*]

Pau, nay, loron plus feu qu'à sang sera,
Laude nager, fuir grand aux surrez,
Les agassas entrée refusera,
Pampon, Durance les tiendra enserrez.

Pau, Nay, Loron more in fire shall the blood be, to swim in praise the great one shall run to the join (of rivers). He shall refuse entry to the magpies. Pampon, Durance shall keep them confined.

This seemingly obscure verse has been interpreted by some commentators as referring to Napoleon Bonaparte and his dealings with the two Popes, Pius VI and Pius VII. If Pau, Nay and Loron are rearranged, it is possible to arrive at Napaulon Roy—'Napoleon King'. The word for magpie in French is *pie* or *pius*, and this would be a play on words typical of Nostradamus.

Napoleon was a considerable thorn in the flesh for Rome and the papacy, and both Pius VI and Pius VII were taken captive by him. Pius VI died in captivity in 1789, and Pius VII was held captive in 1808 but later released.

[*Century 8, quatrain 1*]

1798

Le chef qu'aura conduit peuple infiny
Loing de son ciel, de mœurs & langue estrange
Cinq mil en Grete, & Thessale finy,
Le chef fuyant sauvé en la marine grange.

The leader who shall conduct an infinite number of people, far from their skies to strange manners and language. Five thousand shall be finished in Crete and Thessaly, the leader evasive, saved in a seagoing barn.

Following Napoleon's campaign in Egypt, he was forced to flee in a wooden supply ship (the reference to a barn which was normally built of wood) and successfully landed in France without being intercepted by British naval ships. He left behind a depleted army of 5,000 men who had to face the Turks occupying Crete and Thessaly at that time.

[*Century 1, quatrain 98*]

1798–1802

Dans la Sardaigne un noble Roy viendra,
Qui ne tiendra que trois ans le Royaume,
Plusieurs couleurs avec soy conjoindra,
Luy mesme apres soin somme il marrit scome.

Into Sardinia shall come a noble king who shall only hold the kingdom for three years. He shall join many colours to himself; to himself after care, slumber, affliction, taunts shall come.

King Charles Emmanuel lost much of his land to France and left for Sardinia in 1798, where he ruled for three years. He abdicated (allowing his brother, Victor Emmanuel I, to assume the title) and went into exile in Rome, joining the Jesuit order until his death in 1819.

[*Century 8, quatrain 88*]

1799

Naufrage à classe pres d'onde Hadriatique,
La terre esmeuë sur l'air en terre mis.
Egypte tremble augment Mahommetique,
Heraut se rendre à crier est commis.

A fleet is wrecked near the waves of the Adriatic, the earth trembles, pushed into the air and falling to land again. Egypt trembles, the Mahometan increases; the herald is sent out to cry for surrender.

This is believed to allude to Napoleon's expedition into Egypt in which his forces were defeated by the British on the Nile. The ship commanded by the admiral of the French navy was blown up, and bits of wreckage were strewn across the land. Napoleon went on to besiege the Turkish forces at the city of Acre, although his own soldiers were struck by an epidemic of plague. A herald was despatched, demanding the surrender of the city, but this was refused. Because of the weakness of his own position, Napoleon was forced to lift the siege.

[*Century 2, quatrain 86*]

1799

> *Lou grand cyssame le levera d'albelhos,*
> *Que non sauran don, te signen venguddos,*
> *Denech l'embousq, sou gach sous les tail hos,*
> *Ciutat trahido per cinq lengos non nudos.*

The great swarm of bees shall rise up, but no one will know from whence they came. The ambush by night, the jay beneath the climbing vines, the city betrayed by five tongues, not naked.

The 'swarm of bees' refers to Napoleon as this was one of the emblems he used (Napoleon's residences at Fontainbleau and Malmaison have carpets and soft furnishings decorated with bees). This quatrain describes the coup d'état of 9 November 1799 in which Napoleon effectively seized control of France and later became emperor. The 'five tongues not naked' refer to the Directoire ('the Directory'—the body of five directors in power in France overthrown by Napoleon), two of whom were in the conspiracy while the other three were bribed. Plans for the coup were finalized the night before, and the action itself was completely successful. The original *les tail hos*, which is translated as 'vines' or 'trellis', is usually regarded as an anagram for the Tuileries, the palace into which Napoleon moved following the coup.

[*Century 4, quatrain 26*]

> *La Royne Ergaste voyant sa fille blesme,*
> *Par un regret dans l'estomach enclos,*
> *Crys lamentables seront lors d'Angolesme,*
> *Et au germain mariage forclos.*

The Queen Ergaste, seeing her pale daughter, by a regret contained in her stomach. Then lamentable cries will come from Angoulême, and the marriage to the cousin will be denied.

The 'Queen Ergaste' in this quatrain is taken by many to refer to Marie Antoinette. 'Ergaste' seems to have a dual meaning, both 'captive' and 'suffering the manual labour of a penitentiary'. Marie Antoinette was imprisoned and forced to sew her clothes. Her daughter was Madame Royale, who married the Duke of Angoulême in 1799. The marriage was childless ('regret contained in her stomach'), and her 'pale' countenance could no doubt be caused by the problems that beset her family.

[*Century 10, quatrain 17*]

1799 or 1981

Romain Pontife garde de t'aprocher,
De la cité qui deux fleuves arrouse;
Ton sang viendras aupres de la cracher
Toy & les tiens quand fleurira la rose.

Roman Pontiff beware of approaching near the city watered by two rivers. You shall spit blood in that place, both you and yours, when the rose is blooming.

This refers to the death of Pope Pius VI who was taken prisoner in 1799, along with thirty-two of his fellow priests, following the defeat of Rome by the French under Napoleon. The Pope died in August of that year (when the roses were in flower) having been vomiting and spitting blood. The two rivers referred to are the Saône and Rhône, and the Pope was imprisoned at Valence. 'You and yours' alludes to the priests captured with him.

Other commentators have linked this quatrain with the more recent attempted assassination of Pope John Paul II in 1981. A bullet wound caused abdominal bleeding, and the Pope brought up a considerable amount of blood.

[*Century 2, quatrain 97*]

1800

Gaulois par sauts, monts viendra penetrer,
Occupera le grand lieu de l'Insubre;
Au plus profond son ost fera entrer,
Gennes, Monech pousseront classe rubre.

The French by leaping shall penetrate over the mountains and shall occupy the great seat of Insubria. He shall make his army enter deeply. Genoa and Monaco shall have pushed out the red fleet.

This quatrain describes events that occurred in 1800. Early in May of that year, Napoleon took an army of 40,000 men across the Alps via the St Bernard Pass and launched an attack on the Austrians, who were gaining ground in Italy. He overthrew them at Milan (Insubria) on 1 June. Monaco was blockaded and attacked by the British fleet on 23 May, while Genoa was besieged and defeated by Austria on 4 June. However, the Austrians were finally driven out by French forces, and Napoleon returned to Paris in triumph to be hailed as a hero.

[*Century 4, quatrain 37*]

1801–1814

Bien contiguë des grands monts Pyrenées,
Un contre l'aigle grand copie addresser;
Ouvertes vaines, forces exterminées,
Que jusque à Pau, le chef viendra chasser.

Very near the great mountains of the Pyrenees, a man will raise a great army against the eagle. Veins will be opened and strength shall be dissipated. The leader will chase them as far as the Pau.

These lines describe the march by the British army, under the command of General Arthur Wellesley, who later became the Duke of Wellington, through Portugal and Spain and on into France via the Pyrenees. The 'eagle' is Napoleon, although when Wellington led his army into Madrid in 1812, the emperor was otherwise engaged in Russia. The French forces were driven back relentlessly. The supply lines of their army were cut ('veins opened and strength dissipated'), and they were forced to retreat back to the River Pau.

[*Century 4, quatrain 70*]

1805

Entre deux mers dressera promontoire
Que puis mourra par le mords du cheval,
Le sien Neptune pliera voille noire,
Par Calpre & classe aupres de Rocheval.

Between two seas a promontory will stand; by him who will die by the bit of a horse. Neptune will fold a black sail for his own by Gibraltar, and a fleet shall be near Rocheval (Cape Roche).

A number of features surrounding this quatrain describe well the Battle of Trafalgar. The two seas are the Atlantic and the Mediterranean, and the promontory is therefore Gibraltar. The battle was fought between Gibraltar and Cape Roche (otherwise called Rocheval), and the person who dies 'by the bit of a horse' is Villeneuve, the admiral of the French fleet. He was taken captive by the British but was released in 1806. He returned to France, but on his way to report to Napoleon he committed suicide. Admiral Nelson was, of course, killed during the battle by the bullet of a French sniper. On the homeward voyage a black sail was hoisted as a mark of respect.

[*Century 1, quatrain 77*]

1807

Milan, Ferrare, Turin & Aquilleye,
Capne Brundis vexez par gent Celtique,
Par le Lyon & phalange aquilee,
Quand Rome aura le chef vieux Britannique.

Milan, Ferrare, Turin and Aquilia, Capua and Brindisi shall be vexed by the Celtic nation; by the lion and phalanx of the eagle, when Rome shall have the old British chief.

This quatrain may describe the situation in 1807 when Napoleon and the French held power in all the parts of Italy that are mentioned. In the year 1807, the last of the Stuart royal house, Cardinal York, died in Rome—'the old British chief' whose forebears had been monarchs in England and Scotland.

[*Century 5, quatrain 99*]

1808

En navigant captif prins grand pontife;
Grands apprestez saillir les clercs tumultuez,
Second esleu absent son bien debise,
Son favory bastard à mort tué.

In sailing the great Pope shall be taken captive, great uproar amongst the troubled clergy. The second elected absent, his goodness debased, his favourite bastard put to death.

These lines seem to allude to the imprisonment, in 1808, of Pope Pius VII by the French forces of Napoleon Bonaparte and the subsequent capture of Rome itself. The clergy were 'troubled' and in 'uproar', both before and after this event because the Catholic Church had been abolished. Pius VII had in fact travelled to Paris in 1804 to crown Napoleon as emperor, so this act would have seemed even more infamous. 'The second elected absent' may refer to Pope Pius VI, who was exiled and died in Valence as a direct result of Napoleon's activities. The 'favourite bastard' is Napoleon himself (an illegitimate claimant to the throne of France). Perhaps the 'favourite' refers to the fact that he was acknowledged and crowned as emperor by the Pope. (*See also* 1797, page 107.)

[*Century 5, quatrain 15*]

1809–1865

La sacree pompe viendra baisser les aisles
Par la venuë du grand Legislateur;
Humble haussera, vexera les rebelles,
Naistra sur terre aucun semulateur.

The sacred pomp shall come to lower her wings, at the coming of the great lawgiver. He will raise the humble and vex the rebellious, no one to emulate him shall be born again on earth.

This quatrain appears to describe Abraham Lincoln, who was born in 1809 and is arguably the greatest president to have graced that office in the United States of America. He rose from exceedingly humble origins to the greatest position in the land and strove throughout his life for 'freedom and justice for all'.

[*Century 5, quatrain 79*]

1810–1814 see 1625–1649

1812

Terroir Romain qu'interpretoit augure,
Par gens Gauloise par trop sera vexee,
Mais nation Celtique craindra l'heure,
Boreas, classe trop loing l'avoir poussee.

1812

Roman land that is interpreted by the augur, will be greatly vexed by the French nation. But the Celtic nation will be afraid of the hour of the north wind, having driven their fleet too far.

Italy ('Roman land') suffered at the hands of Napoleon's armies, and in 1810 the papal states of the Vatican were subjugated. The last lines of the quatrain appear to allude to the disastrous Russian campaign in 1812, in which the bitter winter weather ('the north wind') caused severe hardship and losses among Napoleon's army. Only one tenth of a force of over 450,000 returned home to France. The 'fleet' driven 'too far' may refer to the earlier defeat of Napoleon's fleet by the British at the Battle of Trafalgar in 1805.

[*Century 2, quatrain 99*]

Vent Aquilon fera partir le siege,
Par murs jetter cendres, chaulx & poussiere,
Par pluye apres qui leur fera bien piege,
Dernier secours encontre leur frontiere.

The north wind will cause the siege to be raised, over the walls, cinders, lime and dust thrown; afterwards, by rain which is a scourge to them, the last help is encountered against the frontier.

Most commentators apply this to the capture of Moscow in 1812 and the subsequent burning of the old city. The French army were forced to retreat and thousands died from their wounds or as a result of the weather. The survivors, who had been abandoned by Napoleon, only found help when they reached the border of the empire and were on their way home.

[*Century 9, quatrain 99*]

1812–1813

Amas s'approche venant d'Esclavonie,
L'Olestant vieux cité ruynera,
Fort desolee verra sa Romanie,
Puis la grand flamme estaindre ne sçaura.

A massed army shall approach from Slavonia, the destroyer will ruin the old city; he will see his Roman empire quite desolated, then will not know how to extinguish the great flame.

This quatrain describes Napoleon's troubled march through Russia and the capture of the abandoned 'old city' of Moscow. On 14 September 1812, a few Russian patriots set fire to the old wooden city, and the French army were powerless to stop the flames. The 'great flame' may also allude to the subsequent battles and warfare waged by those countries that united against Napoleon and eventually brought about his downfall. The 'Roman empire' (*Romanie* in the French) possibly refers to the dynasty that Napoleon had hoped would stem from him, and his baby son was in fact given the title of King of Rome. Napoleon lived to see all his hopes brought to nothing, as is described in this quatrain.

[*Century 4, quatrain 82*]

1812 or 1815

Prest à combattre fera defection,
Chef adversaire obtiendra la victoire,
L'arriere garde fera defention,
Les deffaillans mort au blanc territoire.

He who was ready to fight will desert, the chief adversary will obtain the victory. The rear guard will make a defence, those faltering dying in a white country.

This quatrain refers once again to the defeats suffered by Napoleon. It can be attributed to his disastrous retreat from Russia, in which all but a few thousand of the army perished as a direct result of the fighting or from hunger and cold. Napoleon disguised himself and returned to France ahead of his troops, leaving them to manage as best they could in a snow-covered land ('white country'). It is this desertion that may be alluded to in the very first line of the quatrain.

Alternatively, the quatrain could be said to describe Napoleon's defeat at Waterloo. In this case, the one who deserts is Marshal Grouchy, who delayed and failed to implement Napoleon's orders. The chief victorious adversary is the Duke of Wellington and Napoleon's fanatically loyal Imperial Guard fought until all were dead. The 'white country' in this case may be a reference to the many white cockades (emblem of the Bourbon royal line) that were displayed in Paris following Napoleon's capture. The subsequent return of Louis XVIII, Charles X and Louis Philippe to the throne restored the Bourbons for a brief period during the early part of the 1800s.

[*Century 4, quatrain 75*]

1813–1814

L'aigle posee entour des pavillons,
Par autres oyseaux d'entour sera chassee,
Quand bruit des cymbres, tubes et sonnaillons,
Rendront le sens de la Dame insensee.

The eagle pushed back around the tents shall be chased by other birds surrounding him. Then the noise of cymbals, trumpets and bells shall return sense to the insane lady.

'The eagle' refers to Napoleon during his ill-judged Russian campaign when he was driven back from Moscow by the 'other birds', which are Russia, Prussia and Austria. The 'insane woman' may be Josephine, Napoleon's first wife, whom he divorced in order to marry Marie Louise of Austria. Alternatively, the line may refer to the madness of France in allowing this campaign and defeat to happen. The 'return of sense' would then be a reference to the exiling of Napoleon and the eventual restoration of King Louis XVIII.

[*Century 2, quatrain 44*]

1814

Les cinq estrangers entrez dedans le temple
Leur sang viendra la terre prophaner;
Aux Thoulouseins sera bien dure exemple
D'un qui viendra les loix exterminer.

The five foreign ones having entered the temple, their blood will profane the ground. To the Toulousians it shall be a very hard example, made by the one who came to wipe out their laws.

This quatrain is understood to refer to the Battle of Toulouse in 1814. The 'five foreign ones' are Britain, Prussia, Russia, Spain and Austria, who together put an end to Napoleon's military ambition. The land of France was profaned by their presence, and the Duke of Wellington led the English forces in the hard-fought battle for Toulouse, with great loss of life. The allied forces were the 'one who came to wipe out their laws' and who put an end to the rule of France by Napoleon.

[*Century 3, quatrain 45*]

1814

> *Heureux au regne de France heureux de vie,*
> *Ignorant sang, mort fureur & rapine,*
> *Par non flateurs seras mis en envie,*
> *Roy desrobé trop de foy en cuisine.*

Happy in the kingdom of France, happy with life, ignorant of blood, death, fury and taking by force. By a flattering name shall be envied, a king robbed, too much faith in food.

There seems to be an agreement in the interpretation of this quatrain. It refers to Louis XVIII, who was a glutton, enjoying food and wine to excess. He came to the throne in 1814 when Napoleon was exiled on Elba but fled when Napoleon escaped. After the famous hundred days, Louis came back to the throne for a further ten years. The 'flattering name' given to him was Louis de Desiré.

[*Century 10, quatrain 16*]

> *Gaulois qu'empire par guerre occupera,*
> *Par son beau frere mineur sera trahy,*
> *Par cheval rude voltigeant trainera,*
> *Du fait le frere long temps sera hay.*

A Frenchman who will occupy an empire by war, will be betrayed by his younger brother in law. He will be dragged along by a rough, excitable horse; for the act the brother will be long hated.

This quatrain relates to a relative by marriage of Napoleon. His younger sister, Caroline, married the King of Naples, Joachim Murat, who in 1814 betrayed Napoleon. However, in 1815, he took Napoleon's side. The acquisition of power through Napoleon's position was a common feature among his relatives, and Murat was no exception.

[*Century 10, quatrain 34*]

1815

Au peuple ingrat faictes les remonstrances,
Par lors l'armée se saisira d'Antibe,
Dans l'arc Monech feront les doleances,
Et à Frejus l'un l'autre prendra ribe.

To the ungrateful people, remonstrances are made, at that time will the army seize Antibes. Within the arch of Monaco will the complaints be made and at Frejus one from the other will take the shore.

Louis XVIII urged the people of France to show loyalty to the new regime before leaving for England in 1815, but it was only in Antibes that support for Napoleon held firm. Napoleon himself left for Elba in that same year and both he and the king embarked from near Frejus.

[*Century 10, quatrain 23*]

Le sol & l'aigle au victeur paroistront,
Response vaine au vaincu l'on asseure,
Par cor ne cris harnois n'arresteront,
Vindicte paix, par mort l'acheve à l'heure.

The sun and the eagle will appear to the victor. A vain answer is given to the defeated. Neither by horn nor by cries will the soldiers be stopped. Peace will be through death if achieved in time.

This quotation seems to tie in well with the others that relate to this year, and the same incident, the Battle of Waterloo. This provides a neat continuation from Century 1, quatrain 23 (*see* page 126), as it describes the latter stages of the battle. 'The eagle' refers to the imperial eagle of Napoleon, which would have been visible in the late sunshine when the soldiers advanced.

1815

Napoleon's Imperial Guard were cut down by the fire of the British infantry. The French thought aid was on its way, but it turned out to be the Prussian troops of Marshal Blücher, which resulted in many French soldiers fleeing and they could not be convinced to return ('neither by horn nor cries...'). Peace returned to Europe by the political 'death' of Napoleon.

[*Century 1, quatrain 38*]

> *Par grands dangers le captif eschappé,*
> *Peu de temps grand la fortune changee.*
> *Dans le palais le peuple est attrapé,*
> *Par bon augure la Cité assiegee.*

The captive escaped from great dangers, in a little time his fortune greatly changed. In the palace the people are trapped, by good sign the city besieged.

The 'captive' referred to here is Napoleon who escaped, not without considerable risk, from Elba on 1 March 1815. ('Fortune greatly changed' may refer either to this or to the reversal in Napoleon's fortunes that was to follow with the Battle of Waterloo in 1915.) Napoleon's enthusiastic supporters swept him into Paris and carried him in triumph to the royal palace. Sheer weight of numbers of people made it impossible for anyone to enter or leave the palace for some time.

The 'city besieged' may refer to an event farther into the future, when Paris was besieged by the Allies before being liberated during the Second World War.

[*Century 2, quatrain 66*]

> *Par conflit Roy regne abandonnera,*
> *Le plus grand chef faillira au besoing,*
> *Morts profligez, peu en rechappera,*
> *Tous destranchez, un en sera tesmoing.*

By a conflict the king shall abandon his kingdom, the great leader shall fail in time of need. Dead, ruined, few shall escape, all cut off, one alone shall be left a witness.

This quatrain is usually attributed to the defeat of Napoleon at Waterloo. The failed leader may be Marshal de Grouchy, and Napoleon's forces suffered a devastating and decisive defeat. Napoleon was forced to abdicate as emperor and passed his last six years in lonely exile on the island of St Helena in the South Atlantic.

[*Century 4, quatrain 45*]

*Du Bourg la Reyne parviedrot droit a Chartres
Et feront pres du Pont Anthony pause,
Sept pour la paix cauteleux comme Martres
Feront entree d'armes a Paris clause.*

From Bourge la Reine they will come straight to Chartres, and make a stop near the bridge of Anthony. Seven for peace as crafty as Martens, they will make an entry; armed, into a closed Paris.

Yet another quatrain that is attributed to Napoleon. The seven will be the countries who formed an alliance against Napoleon, namely Russia, Britain, Austria, Prussia, Sweden, Spain and Portugal. They entered Paris during July 1815. The French troops left the city for Chartres and, as they did so, passed Bourge la Reine and Anthony's Bridge.

[*Century 9, quatrain 86*]

*Le captif prince aux Itales vaincu
Passera Gennes par mer jusqu'à Marseille,
Par grand effort des forens survaincu,
Sauf coup de feu, barril liqueur d'abeille.*

1815

The captive prince vanquished in Italy, will pass from Genoa by sea to Marseilles. By a great effort of foreigners overcome, save for a shot, a barrel of bees' honey.

Once again Nostradamus is referring to Napoleon, when he escaped from his captivity on Elba. He landed near Marseilles, at Cannes. He was defeated at Waterloo, and the reference to bees' honey recalls his emblem (*see also* 1799, Century 4, quatrain 26, page 110).

[*Century 10, quatrain 24*]

> *Comme un gryphon viendra le Roy d'Europe,*
> *Accompagné de ceux d'Aquilon,*
> *De rouges & blancs conduira grande troppe,*
> *Et iront contre le Roy de Babylon.*

Like a griffin, the King of Europe will come, accompanied by those of the north. He shall conduct a great troop of reds and whites, and they will go against the king of Babylon.

Nostradamus here seems to be alluding to allied forces, even a united states of Europe that will come like a griffin. This clearly refers to the mythical griffin (or gryphon), which had the head and wings of an eagle and the body of a lion. If 1815 is taken as the backdrop, the reds and whites could be the English and Austrian soldiers marching against Napoleon.

An alternative is that Nostradamus is prophesying a united Europe behind the leadership of Russia. This inference is drawn because a griffin is also a mystical being (half-man, half-lion) that was supposed to guard the gold of Russia.

[*Century 10, quatrain 86*]

> *Cent fois mourra le tyran inhumain,*
> *Mis à son lieu scavant & debonnaire,*
> *Tout le senat sera dessoubs sa main,*
> *Fasché sera par malin teméraire.*

A hundred times the inhuman tyrant will die, put in his place a wise man and good-natured man. All the senate will be at his command, he will be angered by a reckless, malignant person.

It seems that the likeliest explanation of this quatrain is that Napoleon is the tyrant who dies a hundred deaths while a captive. The wise and good-natured man (*debonnaire* in the original quatrain) would then be Louis XVIII, who was often referred to as 'le debonnaire'. The trouble hinted at in the last line may be the assassination of the Duke de Berry, who was an heir to the throne. However, this must be thought of as a rather tenuous link.

An alternative explanation proposed by some is that the tyrant refers to Stalin, and although his successor, Khrushchev, may have seemed good-natured by comparison, he too was deposed (by Leonid Brezhnev and Alexei Kosygin).

[*Century 10, quatrain 90*]

1815 see 1812

1815 or 1939–1945

Au moys troisiesme se levant du Soleil,
Sanglier, Liepard aux champs Mars pour combattre.
Liepard laissé, au ciel extend son œil,
Un Aigle autour du soleil voir s'esbatre.

In the third month, at the rising of the sun, the wild boar and the leopard battle in the fields of Mars. The tired leopard lifts his gaze to heaven and sees an eagle flying around the sun.

This has, in recent analyses, become one of the most well known of Nostradamus' quatrains. It is a description of the Battle of Waterloo on 18 June. The plan was for Marshal Blücher and his Prussian troops to meet Wellington at Waterloo, but earlier the Prussians had been beaten back at Ligny and there was a delay in the rendezvous. The 'leopard' is a variant on the English lion, and the English leopard was assaulted all day by the French, until, almost at dusk, Blücher arrived to turn the tide against the French. The 'eagle' probably refers to Napoleon himself and the standards of Napoleon's troops, which, since Wellington was facing south, could have appeared to be flying around the sun. Despite the fact that the battle occurred in June, Nostradamus refers to 'the third month'. This may be a reference to three months after the March solstice or to the three months of Napoleon's reign, which this battle ended.

Although one can see the attraction of this interpretation, an alternative but more general version could be the English leopard battling with the German boar, with the American eagle about to pounce, i.e. a reference to the Second World War.

[*Century 1, quatrain 23*]

1820

Lune obscur cie aux profondes tenebres,
Son frere passe de couleur ferrugine;
Le grand caché long temps soubs les tenebres,
Tiendra fer dans la playe sanguine.

The moon obscured in deepest darkness, his brother becomes blood-coloured. The great one hidden for a long time under the shadows, will hold the iron in the bloody wound.

The 'moon obscured' refers to the Comte d'Artois, a cousin to Louis XVI who was executed. Artois was in exile for a long time but eventually returned to France to become King Charles X. His son was the Duke of Berry, and he was attacked and stabbed at the Paris Opéra by a Bonapartist fanatic. It is said that as he died he held the dagger ('hold the iron') and said, 'I am murdered, I am holding the hilt of the dagger.'

[*Century 1, quatrain 84*]

> *Chef de Fossan aura gorge couppee,*
> *Par le ducteur du limier & leurier,*
> *La fait paré par ceux du mont Tarpee,*
> *Saturne en Leo treziesme Feurier.*

The leader from Fossano will have his throat cut, by the man who exercised the bloodhounds and the greyhounds. The deed will be committed by those of the Tarpean Rock when Saturn is in Leo on the thirteenth of February.

The 'leader from Fossano' is considered by most commentators to be the Duke of Berry, who was the grandson of King Fossano of Sardinia. The duke was assassinated on 13 February 1820 by a man named Louis Pierre Louvel who had fanatical Republican sympathies. This fact is hinted at in the reference to the Tarpean Rock. Convicted criminals were thrown to their death from the top of this cliff as a means of execution during the days of republican Rome. Louvel worked in the stables where both horses and hounds were kept. He fatally stabbed the duke on the date mentioned outside the Paris Opéra. As he lay dying, the duke's last words were, 'I am murdered. I am holding the hilt of the dagger'.

[*Century 3, quatrain 96*]

> *Le nepveu grand par forces prouvera,*
> *Le pache fait du cœur pusillanime;*
> *Ferrare & Ast le Duc esprouvera,*
> *Par lors qu'au soir fera la pantomine.*

The nephew shall prove by great force. The crime committed by a pusillanimous heart; the duke shall try Ferrare and Asti; by when the comedy shall be in the evening.

The event described here is the assassination of the Duke de Berry, which occurred when he was leaving an evening performance of comic opera in Paris on 13 February 1820. The nephew is Louis Napoleon Bonaparte (Napoleon III) who became a contender for the throne as a direct result of this murder of the son and heir of Charles X of France (*see* Century 1, quatrain 84 and Century 3, quatrain 96, pages 126 and 127).

[*Century 4, quatrain 73*]

Un serpent veu proche du lit Royal,
Sera par dame, nuict chiens n'abbayeront.
Lors naistre en France un Prince tant Royal
Du ciel venu tous les princes verront.

A snake shall be seen near the royal bed by a lady at night, the dogs will not bark. Then will be born in France a prince so royal that all the princes shall see him as a gift from heaven.

At the time of the assassination of the Duke of Berry in 1820, his wife was in the early stages of pregnancy. Seven months later she gave birth to a son who became Duke of Bordeaux and was Charles X's grandson. The snake is the Duc d'Orléans, who tried to sow seeds of doubt about the child's legitimacy. As a member of the family, the Duc d'Orléans was a trusted visitor to the house so the dogs did not bark. The new heir to the throne was called Dieudonné ('gift from heaven') by those loyal to the French monarchy.

[*Century 4, quatrain 93*]

1820–1838

L'arbre qu'estoit par si long temps seché,
Dans une nuict viendra à reverdir;
Son Roy malade, prince pied estaché,
Craint d'ennemis fera voiles bondir.

The tree which had been long dead and withered shall, in the night, flourish again. The king his grandfather will be sickly, the prince has a withered foot. Fear of his enemies shall make him run up sail.

The 'tree which had been long dead and withered' referred to in this quatrain may be the Duke of Berry who was assassinated in 1820. The 'flourishing again at night' alludes to the birth of his son seven months after the murder on 29 September of that year. This child, the Duke of Bordeaux, was heir to the throne of France and suffered a riding accident in 1841, which left him permanently lame. However, he was destined never to claim the throne but spent most of his life in exile along with his elderly grandfather, Charles X. By the mid-1800s, France had firmly rejected the monarchy and established a republic under its president, and later emperor, Louis Napoleon Bonaparte.

[*Century 3, quatrain 91*]

1820–1846

Du vray rameau des fleurs de lys issu,
Mis & logé heritier d'Herutrie;
Son sang antique de longue main yssu,
Fera Florence florir en l'armoirie.

Issued from the true branch of the fleur de lys, placed and lodged as heir to Etruria; his ancient blood a long time spun by hands, shall make the coat of arms of Florence flourish.

Another quatrain describing Henri de Bourbon, the Duke of Bordeaux (Count of Chambord), who was born in 1820 seven months after the assassination of his father, the Duke of Berry. He was the grandson and heir of Charles X of France but was forced to live in exile in Italy ('Etruria'). Hence he was 'the true branch of the fleur de lys'. In 1846 he married into the house of Florence, which also had the fleur de lys as part of its coat of arms. His bride was the daughter of Duke Francis IV of Florence and their marriage enabled both family lines to continue to flourish. During the duke's lifetime, France became firmly established as a republic so that he was destined never to ascend the throne and died in exile, as did his grandfather (*see also* Century 4, quatrain 93 on page 128 and Century 3, quatrain 73, below).

[*Century 5, quatrain 39*]

1820–1871

Quand dans le regne parviendra le boiteux,
Compediteur aura proche bastard,
Luy & le regne viendront si fort rogneux,
Qu'ains qu'il guerisse son fait sera bien tard.

When the lame man comes into the kingdom he will have a bastard as a near competitor. Both he and the kingdom will become so much trimmed down, that before he recovers, his action will be too late.

This verse may describe the Duke of Bordeaux, who was heir to the throne of France after Charles X. He suffered a riding accident in 1841, which left him lame, and he had an illegal (hence 'bastard') rival for the throne in the person of the Count of Paris. France was greatly 'trimmed down' as a result of the Franco-Prussian War. The Duke of Bordeaux came too late because, by 1848, France had rejected the old monarchy for ever and declared a second republic. Its president was a nephew of Napoleon Bonaparte, Louis Napoleon Bonaparte, who assumed the title of Emperor Napoleon III. He remained in power from 1852 to 1871 while both the Duke of Bordeaux and the Count of Paris passed the remainder of their lives as exiles.

[*Century 3, quatrain 73*]

1830

De nuict, dans le lict, le supresme estrange,
Pour trop avoir suborné blond esleu,
Par trois l'Empire subroge exancle,
A mort mettra carte ne pacquet leu.

By night, in bed, the chief one will be strangled, for having become too involved with the blond (heir) elect. By three the Empire is enslaved and replaced. He is put to death, reading neither letter nor packet.

This is a somewhat ambiguous quatrain that can be interpreted in a number of ways and even then with different emphases. The likeliest option is that it refers to Louis, Prince of Condé, who was found hanged (not 'strangled') in his bedroom. He was the last of the line, hence the use of the word 'chief'. The 'blond elect' could have at least two meanings, either a blonde mistress or it may pertain to the Duke of Bordeaux, who was heir to the French throne. The 'three' could well be those who plotted against the Condés, who included Charles X. It is known that Condé's will was rewritten in favour of the Duke of Bordeaux, and it is probably this that is referred to in the last part of this quatrain.

[*Century 1, quatrain 39*]

1830–1848

Sept ans sera Philip fortune prospere,
Rabaissera des Barbares l'effort,
Puis son midi perplex revours affaire,
Jeune Ogmion abysmera son fort.

Seven years will Philip have prosperous fortune, he will beat down the efforts of the barbarians. Then at his height, perplexed with conflicting affairs, young Ogmion will put down his strength.

The early part of this quatrain fits well with Louis Philippe of France, although the ending is less clear. In the first seven years of his reign, fortune favoured Philippe and he subdued the 'barbarians' (the Arabs in some interpretations) while also securing Algeria. His reign ended in 1848 with the proclamation of the new republic.

Alternatively, it could refer to Philip II of Spain, acknowledged as being the first sovereign to rule an 'absolute' monarchy. His was the dominant power in Europe (he reigned from 1556 to 1598), and he controlled southern Italy and Sicily and conquered Portugal. In attempting to own a massive empire, Philip inevitably ignored the more mundane aspects of government ('perplexed with conflicting affairs'?) and proved that one could not govern far-flung territories with a totally centralized system.

[*Century 9, quatrain 89*]

1831–1848 and 1852–1871

Apres le siege tenu dix sept ans,
Cinq changeront en tel revolu terme,
Puis sera l'un esleu de mesme temps,
Qui des Romains ne sera trop conforme.

After the seat has been held for seventeen years, five shall change in such a space of time; then one will be elected at the same time who the Romans shall not be very comfortable with.

King Louis-Philippe of France reigned for seventeen years and was the father of five sons. He was driven into exile, an object of ridicule, in 1848, and his successor, Louis Napoleon Bonaparte (Napoleon III), was elected as leader in 1852. In view of all that had occurred before, probably many European nations, and not just the Italians, viewed the election of Emperor Napoleon III with unease and disquiet.

[*Century 5, quatrain 92*]

1837–1901 or **Reign of Queen Elizabeth II**

Le regne humain d'Angelique geniture,
Fera son regne paix union tenir,
Captive guerre demy de sa closture,
Long temps la paix leur fera maintenir.

The humane reign of English offspring will cause his reign to be peaceful and united. War captive, half in his enclosure, for a long time peace will be maintained.

Although a very generalised quatrain, this has been applied to nineteenth-century Britain but it could also apply to the reign of the present queen. However, in both cases, the sex of the monarch is evidently inaccurate and although there has been peace at home, neither reign has been entirely free from war or controversy.

[*Century 10, quatrain 42*]

1842

L'aisné Royal sur coursier voltigeant,
Picquer viendra si rudement courir;
Gueulle, lepée, pied dans l'estrein pleignant,
Trainé, tire, horriblement mourir.

The eldest royal one, mounted on a frisky charger, shall spur so fiercely that it will bolt. Open-mouthed, foot caught in the stirrup, complaining, dragged, pulled to die horribly.

Crown Prince Ferdinand, who was the heir of Louis Philippe of France, suffered an accident exactly as described in this quatrain and died on 13 July 1842.

[*Century 7, quatrain 38*]

1842–1871

Au Roy l'augure sur le chef la main mettre
Viendra prier pour la paix Italique;
A la main gauche viendra changer se Sceptre,
De Roy viendra Empereur pacifique.

The augur shall put his hand on the king's head and pray for peace in Italy. In his left hand he shall come to change the sceptre, from king he will become a peaceful emperor.

This verse probably refers to Louis Napoleon Bonaparte, the nephew of Bonaparte, who became Napoleon III. The 'augur' is either the Pope or another clergyman, and he puts his hand upon Napoleon's head and prays for peace. The changing of the sceptre from one hand to another may be an indication of Napoleon's juggling during his years as emperor to try and keep all sides satisfied. When he became emperor, Napoleon declared that 'the art of empire is peace', which fits well with the last line of the quatrain.

[*Century 5, quatrain 6*]

1846–1873

Au deserteur de la grand forteresse,
Apres qu'aura son lieu abandonné;
Son adversaire fera si grand provesse,
L'Empereur tost mort sera condamné.

To the deserter of the great fortress after he will have abandoned his place, his adversary will show such great prowess that the emperor shall soon be condemned to death.

This quatrain describes events in the life of Louis Napoleon Bonaparte (Napoleon III). In 1846, Louis Napoleon, the nephew of Napoleon Bonaparte, was considered to be such a threat that he was imprisoned for life in the fortress of Ham. However, he managed to escape and fled to England where he lived in exile. By 1848, revolution was once more in the air, and the French people drove out their king, Louis Philippe, who in turn went into exile. In December of that year, Louis Napoleon staged a coup d'état and was voted prince-president of France, later assuming the title of Emperor Napoleon III. He lacked the skills of his uncle in both diplomatic and military matters, and by 1870, France was embroiled in the Franco-Prussian War. Hence the adversary who shows 'such great prowess' is Prussia, and the French forces suffered a devastating defeat at the Battle of Sedan. Napoleon III was once more forced into exile in England, and his death followed soon afterwards in 1873. He was sixty-five.

[*Century 4, quatrain 65*]

1848–1870

Par le decide de deux choses bastars,
Nepveu du sang occupera le regne,
Dedans lectoure seront les coups de dards
Nepveu par pleira l'enseigne.

Through the fall of two bastard things, the nephew of the blood shall occupy the kingdom. Within Lectoure there shall be blows of lances, the nephew through fear shall fold up his ensigns.

In this quatrain, the 'nephew' described is Louis Napoleon III, whose uncle was Napoleon Bonaparte. The 'two bastard things' may be the reign of King Louis Philippe, who was driven out, and the regime of the Second Republic, which came to an end when Napoleon III staged a coup d'état in 1848. 'Lectoure' is an anagram of Le Torcey, which was a part of Sedan where Napoleon III was defeated during the Franco-Prussian Wars in 1870. Napoleon III hung up flags of surrender in Sedan and surrendered to the Prussians, and then went into exile in England, where he remained until his death in 1873.

[*Century 8, quatrain 43*]

1851 and 1791–1793

Esleu sera Renard ne sonnant mot,
Faisant le saint public vivant pain d'orge,
Tyrannizer apres tant à un cop,
Mettant à pied des plus grands sur la gorge.

A fox will be elected without uttering one word, in public appearing saintly living on barley bread; afterwards he will suddenly become tyrannical, placing his foot on the throats of the very great men.

This is another quatrain describing Louis Napoleon III, nephew of Napoleon Bonaparte, who was elected president of France in 1848, following the abdication of Louis Philippe. Presumably he appeared at first to be mild and reserved (he was known as 'le Taciturne') but he soon displayed a more tyrannical side to his nature.

In 1851, the Assembly was dissolved and the Second Empire was ushered in and Napoleon III declared himself the new emperor. For all his cunning, his reign ended ignominiously in exile in England and during his twenty years in power, France lost both territory and influence.

[*Century 8, quatrain 41*]

1856

Index & poulse parfondera le front,
De Senegalia le Comte à son fils propre;
La Myrnamée par plusieurs de prin front,
Trois dans sept jours blessez more.

With index finger and thumb he will sprinkle the forehead, the Count of Senigallia will perform this on his true son; Venus by several in short bout, three within seven days are wounded to death.

The baptismal date of the son of Napoleon III was 15 June 1856 and his godfather was Pope Pius IX, himself the son of the Count of Senigallia. However, the three deaths referred to have not been identified and do not apparently have any connection with the baptism described in the opening lines.

[*Century 10, quatrain 8*]

1857

Les exilez deportez dans les Isles,
Au changement d'un plus cruel Monarque,
Seront meurtris, & mis deux des scintilles,
Qui de parler ne seront esté parques.

The exiles deported into the islands at the coming of an ever more cruel monarch, will be murdered; and put into the fire, who were not sparing in their speaking.

A coup d'état in France in 1857 saw many people deported. The new king, Napoleon III, had anyone who spoke against the state deported. Although this fits the basic tenets of the quatrain it is not a particularly strong connection. There are others who ascribe this to the wholesale extermination of the Jews (and the Poles) by Hitler because there is an obvious comment on the mass cremations.

[*Century 1, quatrain 59*]

1858

Un chef Celtique dans le conflit blessé,
Aupres de cave voyant siens mort abbatre;
De sang & playes & d'ennemis pressé,
Et secours par incogneuz de quatre.

A French leader in the conflict wounded, near a theatre sees his subjects about to be felled by death. Harassed by blood, wounds and enemies and saved by unknown ones from the four.

This quatrain describes the attempted assassination of Napoleon III on the night of 14 January 1858 as the emperor left the opera. 'The four' are the Italian revolutionary conspirators responsible for the assassination attempt (named Orsini, Pieri, Rudio and Gomez). Many people were killed and others were injured but Napoleon himself was only slightly wounded. Nostradamus implies that Napoleon may have been saved from the full force of the blast by those around him.

[*Century 5, quatrain 10*]

1859

Delà les Alpes grand armee passera,
Vn peu devant naistra monstre vapin;
Prodigieux & subit tournera,
Le grand Toscan à son lieu plus propin.

Beyond the Alps a great army shall pass, a little while before a wretched monster shall be born. Prodigious and suddenly he shall turn, the great Tuscan shall return to his own nearest place.

This may refer to the crossing of the Alps by the army of Napoleon III in 1859, in which case the 'wretched monster' is the unleashing of the forces of revolution in Italy. The 'great Tuscan' is Leopold II, Grand Duke of Tuscany, who was driven into Austria, his 'nearest place'.

[*Century 5, quatrain 20*]

1870

Feu, couleur d'or du ciel en terre veu,
Frappé du haut n'ay, fait cas merveilleux;
Grand meurtre humain, prinse du grand neveu,
Morts d'expectacles, eschappé l'orgueilleux.

1870–1871

Fire the colour of gold from the sky shall be seen on earth, stricken from the high-born, a marvellous happening. Great murder of humanity, taken from the great one, a nephew; deaths of the spectators, the proud one will escape.

The 'nephew of the great one' is believed to be a reference to Napoleon III, the nephew of Napoleon Bonaparte, who was Emperor of France from 1852 to 1871. The quatrain describes Germany's war with France in 1870, and the opening lines allude to the devastating fire power of the German artillery. There is also a reference to a well-documented incident in August 1870 in which Napoleon narrowly missed death when a bullet landed at his feet. By September of that year, the armies of Otto Von Bismarck, the Prime Minister of Prussia, occupied Paris, France had surrendered, Napoleon III was captured and imprisoned and France shortly after became a republic once more.

[Century 2, quatrain 92]

1870–1871

De feu celeste au Royal edifice,
Quand la lumiere du Mars deffaillira,
Sept mois grand' guerre, mort gent de malefice,
Rouen Eureux, au Roy ne faillira.

Fire shall fall from the sky onto the royal edifice when the light of Mars is failing. For seven months a great war, people dead through malevolence. Rouen and Evreux shall not fail the king.

This quatrain seems to describe events in the Franco-Prussian War, which was waged for seven months, from July 1870 to February 1871. The Tuileries Palace in Paris was devastated by canon fire as the city was besieged. The 'light of Mars failing' may refer to the Bonaparte family (in this case Napoleon III) whose days of glory were finally at an end. Normandy stayed royalist and wished to see the monarchy restored.

[*Century 4, quatrain 100*]

1883–1945

Le grand naistra de Veronne & Vincence,
Qui portera un surnom bien indigne.
Qui à Venise vouldra faire vengeance,
Luy mesme prins homme du guet & signe.

The great one shall be born of Verona and Vincenza, who shall bear a very unworthy surname; he who at Venice will wish to take vengeance, but he himself shall be taken by a man of the watch and sign.

The man of the 'very unworthy surname' is Benito Mussolini, who was born in 1883 not far from the towns mentioned in northern Italy. His surname means literally 'muslin-maker', a humble trade that was not very highly regarded. Mussolini ruthlessly rose to power and maintained his position, by removing those who got in his way, but was himself finally defeated.

[*Century 8, quatrain 33*]

1889

Perdu, trouvé, caché de si long siecle,
Sera pasteur demy Dieu honoré,
Ains que la Lune acheve son grand cycle,
Par autres vents sera deshonoré.

Lost, found, hidden for so many centuries. Pasteur will be honoured, like a god. Thus when the moon achieves her grand century (cycle), by other winds (rumours) he will be dishonoured.

The primary feature of this quatrain is that Pasteur is mentioned by name. This is taken to be Louis Pasteur who, towards the end of the nineteenth century, established the theory that germs are responsible for the transmission of disease. He also discovered a rabies vaccine, a method for protecting cattle and poultry from disease, and similar microbiological advances affecting the silk, wine and beer industries. Pasteur established his Institute in 1889, and the reference to the moon's cycle is taken as an indication of the date of the Institute's founding, because the cycle of the moon finished in 1889. The dishonour refers to the hostility Pasteur received at the hands of the French Academy, many of whom considered him to be a fraud.

[*Century 1, quatrain 25*]

1889–1945

Du plus profond de l'Occident d'Europe,
De pauvres gens un jeune enfant naistra,
Qui par sa langue seduira grande troupe;
Son bruit au regne d'Orient plus croistra.

Out of the deepest part of Western Europe a child shall be born of poor family, who by his tongue shall seduce many peoples. His fame shall increase even more in the kingdom of the Orient.

These lines appear to best describe the rise of Adolf Hitler (although it could possibly be attributed to other historical leaders). Hitler was born into a poor peasant family in Austria and became a hugely charismatic leader who swayed people by his powerful speeches. His reputation was even greater in Japan, which allied itself with Germany during the Second World War.

[*Century 3, quatrain 35*]

> *Aupres du Rin des montagnes Moriques,*
> *Naistra un grand de gens trop tard venu,*
> *Qui deffendra Saurome & Pannoniques,*
> *Qu'on ne sçaura qu'il sera devenu.*

Near the Rhine out of the Norican mountains shall be born a great one of the people, come too late. He shall defend Poland and Hungary so that what becomes of him shall not be known.

This quatrain is nearly always attributed to the life and fate of Adolf Hitler, although some of the lines may seem surprising to present-day readers. Hitler was born in Austria (the 'Norican Mountains') and was 'of the people' in the sense that he was of lowly rather than exalted parentage. In Nostradamus' writings, 'great' often means a person of power and might rather than being linked with qualities of goodness, as it usually is today. 'Come too late' is usually interpreted as meaning that Hitler's plans for conquest and subjugation of other nations were already outdated by the twentieth century. Few people today would accept that Germany's activities in Poland or any other country were anything other than pure aggression and conquest. Nostradamus may have been alluding to propaganda or a wish of Hitler to have it believed that he was trying to 'defend' these countries against the allies. The last line of the verse casts doubt on the eventual fate of Hitler being 'not known'. While few doubt that the bodies charred beyond recognition in the Berlin bunker were those of Hitler and his mistress, Eva Braun, this has always been a subject of speculation.

[*Century 3, quatrain 58*]

1894–1906

Tard arrivé l'execution faite,
Le vent contraire, lettres au chemin prinses;
Les conijurez quatorze d'une secte,
Par le Rosseau seront les entreprinses.

Arrived late, the execution will happen. The wind was contrary and letters intercepted on the way. The conspirators were fourteen of a sect. By Rousseau the enterprises will happen.

The events outlined here fit well with the case of Alfred Dreyfus, a French soldier and a Jew found guilty of treason for selling military secrets to the Germans and shipped to a penal colony (Devil's Island) in 1895. In 1899, he was returned to France for a retrial. Unfortunately, anti-Semitic feelings were strong and he was again convicted. A few days later, he was pardoned by President Emile Loubet, and further investigations were ordered by the court. The individual involved in these investigations was called Rousseau. Rousseau was totally against Dreyfus and not surprisingly had found him guilty, but this decision was destroyed by a public pardon. It was ultimately decided that the letters that had formed the basis of Dreyfus' conviction were forgeries and he was pronounced innocent. In addition to the mention of Rousseau by name in the last line, it seems that proof of Dreyfus' innocence was too 'late' and he would be incarcerated, and the 'contrary wind' can be taken as the anti-Semitic feelings at that time. The implication is that the conspiracy was hatched and perpetrated by a group of fourteen, but there is no evidence to confirm or refute this.

An alternative interpretation, reading 'Rousseau' as 'the red one'. is that this refers to the assassination of the Tsar Nicholas II and his family by Russian revolutionaries in 1918.

[Century 1, quatrain 7]

1912–1917

Par fureur faincte d'esmotion divine,
Sera la femme du grand fort violée;
Juges voulans damner telle doctrine,
Victime au peuple ignorant immolée.

By feigned fury of a divine emotion, the wife of the great one shall be much violated. The judges wish to damn such a doctrine, a victim to the ignorant people is sacrificed.

In this quatrain, Nostradamus appears to be describing the Tsarina Alexandra, wife of Tsar Nicholas II of Russia, and her relationship with the infamous 'monk', Grigori Rasputin. Alexandra was an anxious mother, obsessed with the condition of her only, sickly, haemophiliac son, Alexei. Rasputin gained a hold and influence on Alexandra by apparently managing to cure and comfort the boy during several severe attacks of his illness. Nicholas appears to have welcomed, or at least tolerated, the presence of Rasputin because of the seeming benefit to his son and wife. Rasputin gained ascendancy over the mind of Alexandra, and through her of Nicholas and the affairs of state. This may be the 'violation' referred to, although many at the time suspected that Rasputin and Alexandra were having an affair.

In any event, Russians were scandalized that an ignorant peasant monk, especially one with a known reputation as a drunk and womanizer, should be exercising such control over the running of the country. A plot was hatched among a group of aristocrats to kill Rasputin, and this was carried out in 1916. A 'victim' sacrificed to 'the ignorant people' does not seem very appropriate here, as many believed that this act would save the Romanovs and Russia. Rasputin was a victim, in so far as he died an appalling, prolonged death involving poisoning with cyanide, shooting, beating and eventually, as a last resort, drowning. The manner of his death helped to enhance his reputation as someone who had held a charmed life linked with sorcery and evil.

[*Century 6, quatrain 72*]

1915

Vers Aquitaine par insuls Britanniques,
Et par aux mesmes grandes incursions,
Pluyes, gelees feront terroirs iniques,
Port Selyn fortes fera invasions.

Towards Aquitaine by British assaults, by them also great incursions. Rains and frost make the terrain unsafe. Against Port Selin they will make strong invasions.

This quatrain refers to the period in the First World War when France ('Aquitaine') and Britain were stuck in appalling weather conditions in the trenches on the Western Front. Through the persistence of Winston Churchill, the Allies launched a second front with an attack on the Dardanelles in the hope that this would force the end of the war by splitting the German army. Part of the plan was to capture Constantinople ('Port Selin') but overall the campaign was a disaster for the British forces.

[*Century 2, quatrain 1*]

1918

L'horrible guerre qu'en l'Occident s'appreste;
L'an ensuivant viendra la pestilence,
Si fort horrible que jeune, vieux, ne beste,
Sang, feu, Mercure, Mars, Jupiter en France.

1918

The horrible war prepared in the West, the following year the pestilence will come, so horrible that the young, the old, the beasts (will be smitten), blood, fire, Mercury, Mars, Jupiter in France.

A quatrain that appears to refer to the horrors of the First World War and the influenza pandemic that followed in 1917–1918, that was responsible for the deaths of millions of people. Nostradamus suggests a link with the conjunction of Mercury, Mars and Jupiter and a particular effect in France.

[*Century 9, quatrain 55*]

Quand colomnes de bois grande tremblee,
D'auster conduicte couverte de rubriche,
Tant vuidera dehors une grand assemblee,
Trembler Vienne & le pays d'Austriche.

When the wooden columns shall tremble greatly, by the stern wind, covered with a ruby hue (blood). Such a large assembly shall go out and Vienna and the land of Austria will tremble.

Although this has been associated with Austria in 1918, it could equally well apply to the period from 1934 to 1938. However, it does refer to momentous happenings in any event. In 1918, when the trees ('wooden columns') trembled, a new revolutionary order replaced the autocracy of the Hapsburgs, following demonstrations by workers and students in Vienna, and a republic was declared. The 'large assembly' may refer to the world powers (Triple Entente).

If one looks at the period from 1934 to 1938 in the history of Austria, this quatrain could also be referring to the uprising of 1934, also in Vienna, which preceded the assassination of Engelbert Dollfuss, the Chancellor, and was eventually followed in 1938 by the annexation of Austria by Nazi Germany.

[*Century 1, quatrain 82*]

Des innocens le sang de vefue & vierge,
Tant de maux faicts par moyen de grand Roge,
Saincts simulachres trempez en ardant cierge,
De frayeur craincte ne verra nul que boge.

The blood of innocent ones, widow and virgin. So much wickedness committed by means of the great Red, images of saints placed over candles burning, petrified by fear, none will be seen to move.

This quatrain appears to relate to the assassination of the Russian imperial family, especially the Empress Alexandra and her virgin children, also with references to the Russian Orthodox church.

[*Century 8, quatrain 80*]

1918–1939

Les fleaux passees diminué le monde,
Long-temps la paix, terres inhabitees;
Seur marchera par le ciel, terre, mer & onde,
Puis de nouveau les guerres suscitees.

The curse being past, the world becomes smaller. The peace for a long time, lands inhabited. Everyone will go safely through the sky, by land and sea, then the wars will begin again anew.

In some respects this quatrain could apply to any peaceful period between wars. However, the reference to the world becoming smaller and the clear indication of air travel, puts this firmly in the twentieth century. The 'curse being past' could refer to disease or equally to war and 'the peace' could be the period between the First and Second World Wars. Travelling 'through the sky' could refer to the first efforts at flying, i.e. at the turn of the century, or, perhaps more likely, to thirty years or so later when flying was a little more commonplace.

[*Century 1, quatrain 63*]

1920s

Les simulachres d'or et d'argent enflez,
Qu'apres le rapt lac au feu furent jettez,
Au descouvert estaincts tous & troublez,
Au marbre escripts, perscripts interiettez.

The simulations of gold and silver inflated, which following the theft were thrown into the lake; at the time of the discovery, all is exhausted and troubled by the debt. All scripts and bonds will be dissolved.

This complex quatrain has been interpreted by some as referring to inflation, paper money and the financial collapse that occurred in the 1920s. However, some believe that the reference to theft and money being thrown into a lake may relate to Nazi plunder during the Second World War and goods that were never recovered by their rightful owners.

[*Century 8, quatrain 28*]

1920–1947

Du Lac Leman, les sermons fascheront,
Des jours seront reduicts par les sepmaines,
Puis mois, puis an, puis tous deffailliront,
Les Magistrats damneront les loix vaines.

The sermons of the Leman lake will be troublesome, the days will extend into weeks, then into months, then into years, when all will fail. The magistrates will condemn their own useless laws.

This seems to fit ideally the creation and ultimate demise of the League of Nations. The 'Leman lake' is the old name for Lake Geneva, and the headquarters of the League were in Geneva. It was set up because of pressure from President Woodrow Wilson of the United States (although the USA did not join), and from its first meeting in 1920 did successfully intervene in some disputes, thus averting further conflict. However, the organization became dominated by pointless arguments and ultimately failed, formally ceasing in 1947, although its end effectively came many years previously.

[*Century 1, quatrain 47*]

1922

Premier grand fruict le Prince de Pesquiere,
Mais puis viendra bien & cruel malin,
Dedans Venise perdra sa gloire fiere,
Et mis à mal par plus joyue Celin.

The first great fruit, the Prince of Pescheria, but then shall come one very cruel and malicious; in Venice he shall lose his fierce pride and is led into evil by young Selin.

Mussolini formed his Fascist Blackshirt movement in 1919. It was opposed by a diverse group of people and there was a considerable amount of fighting. The first notable success that

Mussolini had was to secure a mandate from Victor Emmanuel III, Prince of Pescheria, to form a coalition government. Within three years this government no longer existed and Mussolini had imposed a total hardline dictatorship. Nostradamus says that Mussolini will have his power curtailed in Venice and seemed to foresee (incorrectly) some connection with the crescent moon (Selin) of Turkey.

[*Century 8, quatrain 31*]

Qui ouvrira le monument trouvé,
Et ne viendra le serrer promptement,
Mal luy viendra, & ne pourra prouvé
Si mieux doit estre Roy Breton ou Normand.

He that shall open the tomb when it is discovered and who does not come and shut it promptly; evil shall come to him and no one will be able to prove it. It might have been better to have been an English or Norman king.

Hollywood film-makers have often exploited the theme of the so-called 'curse of the Pharaohs'—the evil or death that supposedly falls on anyone who disturbs the tombs of the ancient Egyptians. Some analysts have linked this quatrain with the strange and mysterious misfortunes that attended archaeologist Howard Carter and his family and his patron, the Earl of Carnarvon, following the discovery and excavation of the tomb of Tutankhamen in the Valley of the Kings in 1922. Lord Carnarvon died quite suddenly before the excavation was completed, and because of ill health Carter was never able to complete a full report on the excavation.

[*Century 9, quatrain 7*]

1925–1944

Aux profligez de paix les ennemis,
Apres avoir l'Italie supperee;
Noir sanguinaire, rouge sera commis,
Feu, sang verser, eau de sang coloree.

To the vanquished the enemies of peace, after they shall have overcome Italy, the bloody black one, red shall be committed, fire and blood shall be shed, water coloured with blood.

This quatrain appears to describe very accurately the rise to power of Mussolini and the Blackshirts—the members of his Italian Fascist party—and the warfare and bloodshed that took place in Italy during this period.

[*Century 6, quatrain 38*]

1933

Un grand Capitaine de la grand Germanie,
Se viendra rendre par simule secours,
A Roy des Roys ayde de Pannonie,
Que sa revolte fera de sang grand cours.

A captain of the great Germany will come to give back by pretending help. A king of kings, the help of Hungary, his revolt (war) will cause great bloodshed.

It is tempting, and probably acceptable, to place this quatrain in Germany at the time of Hitler's rise to power, followed by his domination of Germany and subsequent invasion of Europe. The 'great Germany' undoubtedly equates with the Third Reich and the pretence of help is surprisingly accurate as he invaded

Poland supposedly to give help. For a brief spell, Hitler was indeed 'king of kings', and he captured Hungary. The 'revolt', or war, referring to the Second World War, caused 'great bloodshed', killing as it did millions of soldiers and civilians.

[*Century 9, quatrain 90*]

1933–1940

Quand le plus grand emportera le pris,
De Nuremberg, d'Auspurg, & ceux de Basle,
Par Agripine chef Frankfort repris,
Traverseront par Flamans jusqu'en Gale.

When the greatest one carries off the prize of Nuremberg, of Ausberg and those of Basle, by the leader of Cologne, Frankfurt retaken, they shall go through Flanders as far as France.

The most likely explanation of this quatrain is that it refers to Hitler's rise to power and the beginning of the Second World War. Hitler's power increased during the Nuremberg Rallies (from 1933 to 1939) and in 1936 he assumed control of the Rhineland. In May 1940, Hitler began his aggression against Belgium and Holland (Flanders) and later he engulfed France.

[*Century 3, quatrain 53*]

1933–1945

De la partie de Mammer grand pontife,
Subjuguera les confins du Dannube;
Chasser les croix par fer raffe ne riffe,
Captif, or, bagues, plus de cent mille rubes.

1934–1940

By the warlike party the great pontiff who shall subjugate the borders of the Danube. They shall pursue the iron crosses by hook or by crook, captives, gold, jewels, more than one hundred thousand rubies.

The 'great pontiff' may seem an unlikely name for Hitler, but he is apparently the one described here, along with the Nazi party and their emblem of the crooked iron cross or swastika. The last line describes the countless people who were taken prisoner and their gold, jewels and possessions—all of which were stolen by the Nazis.

[*Century 6, quatrain 49*]

1934–1938 see 1918

1934–1940

Pres du grand fleuve grand fosse terre egeste,
En quinze part sera l'eau divisee;
La cité prinse, feu, sang, cris, conflit mestre,
Et la plus part concerne au collisee.

Near the great river, a great ditch, earth dug out, in fifteen parts the water shall be divided; The city taken, fire, blood, cries, conflict given and the greater part concerned with the collision.

This verse is usually taken to describe the Maginot Line, a defensive wall completed in 1934 along the border of France and Germany. The Maginot Line was an ambitious civil engineering project comprising a number of underground fortresses linked by a subterranean railway. The structure was interrupted by rivers in fifteen places, as described in the quatrain. In fact, the Maginot Line was virtually useless in repelling the German Occupation forces during the Second World War, and the consequences of this were the battles that raged in and around France. Some have suggested that the existence of this quatrain prompted Abbé Torné-Chavigny in the nineteenth century to press for the building of the wall.

[*Century 4, quatrain 80*]

1936 see 1565

1936

Regne en querelle aux freres divisé,
Prendre les armes & le nom Britannique,
Tiltre d'Anglican sera tard advisé,
Surprins de nuict mener à l'air Gallique.

A kingdom in a quarrel by two brothers divided, to take the arms and the name of Britain. The Anglican title shall be advised to guard himself, surprised by night one is carried to the French air.

Nostradamus may have been predicting the controversy surrounding the abdication of King Edward VIII in 1936. Edward's action caused uproar and bitterness in the royal family, and George VI felt ill prepared to become king. Edward fled to France to begin a new life with Mrs Simpson.

[*Century 8, quatrain 58*]

Pour ne vouloir consentir au divorce,
Qui puis apres sera cogneu indigne,
Le Roy des Isles sera chassé par force,
Mis à son lieu qui de Roy n'aura signe.

For not wishing to consent to divorce, which then afterwards will be seen as unworthy, the King of the Islands will be forced to leave, and put in his place one who has no sign of being a king.

This is a surprisingly accurate quatrain when applied to the abdication of Edward VIII in 1936. In December 1936, Edward decided to abdicate after just eleven months as king in order that he might marry the twice-divorced American, Mrs Wallis Simpson. The abdication was not popular, and Edward had to leave Britain because of Mrs Simpson's lack of social status. Thus it was that George VI, who was not in line for the throne, was made king. George subsequently died prematurely at the age of fifty-six, and the widowed Queen Mother, Elizabeth, referred to Mrs Simpson as 'the woman who killed my husband'.

[*Century 10, quatrain 22*]

> *Le jeune nay au regne Britannique,*
> *Qu'aura le pere mourant recommandé,*
> *Iceluy mort Lonole donra topique,*
> *Et à son fils le regne demandé.*

The young man born to the British Kingdom, whom his dying father shall have recommended. Once he is dead, London will give him a topic, and will demand the kingdom back from his son.

Here is another reference to the abdication of Edward VIII in 1936, and the coming to the throne of his brother, George VI. The reference to 'London will give him a topic' almost certainly alludes to the scandal that his association with Mrs Simpson caused.

[*Century 10, quatrain 40*]

> *Du plus profond de l'Espagne enseigne,*
> *Sortant du bout & des fins de l'Europe,*
> *Troubles passant aupres du pont de Laigne,*
> *Sera deffaicte par bande sa grand troppe.*

From the deepest parts of old Spain, coming out from the ends and borders of Europe. Troubles passing next to the bridge of Laigne, his great troop will be defeated by groups of men.

The Spanish Civil War broke out in 1936, and this quatrain reflects the involvement of many nationalities in the conflict ('from the ends and borders of Europe'). The Germans and Italians supported one side, and the Russians the other. The town of Laignes, near Dijon, was occupied by the Germans. The last part of the quatrain could be referring to their defeat ultimately at the hands of the Allies in the Second World War, which followed the Spanish conflict.

[*Century 10, quatrain 48*]

1936–1939

L'un des plus grands fuyra aux Espagnes,
Qu'en longue playe apres viendra seigner,
Passant copies par les hautes montaignes,
Devastant tout & puis en paix regner.

One of the greatest will fly to Spain which will long bleed with a great wound. Troops will pass over high mountains devastating all, and then in peace he will reign.

Prior to 1936, General Franco had been sent as an exile to be military governor of the Canary Islands. He returned to Spain via Morocco, travelling at first by plane (Nostradamus refers to flight), and then across the Mediterranean Sea. His return heralded the start of the Spanish Civil War with its enormous suffering and loss of life (the 'great wound'). Over half a million people were killed or injured in the conflict. The troops who 'passed over high mountains' consisted of 50,000 Italians and 10,000 Germans, who fought for the Nationalists and Franco, and 20,000 Russians and others loyal to the government side. In order to join in the conflict they had to cross the high Pyrenees. After the Civil War, Spain enjoyed a measure of peace in that she remained neutral during the Second World War.

[*Century 3, quatrain 54*]

> *De castel Franco sortira l'assemblée,*
> *L'ambassadeur non plaisant fera scisme;*
> *Ceux de Ribiere seront en la meslée,*
> *Et au grand goulphre desnier ont l'entrée.*

From Castille, Franco shall go out to the Assembly, the ambassador shall not be agreeable and schism shall occur. Those of Rivera shall be in the mêlée, and he shall be denied entry into the great gulf.

This is regarded by many commentators as being one of Nostradamus' most remarkable quatrains. It names both the fascist dictator Francisco Franco and also Primo de Rivera who led the right-wing government in Spain from 1923 to 1936. The 'mêlée' was, of course, the Spanish Civil War. Franco had been exiled to the Canary Islands when, in 1933, a right-wing government led by Rivera was in power. Left-wing groups, liberals, nationalist minorities and intellectuals rebelled against the repressive regime, and in 1936 a left-wing government came to power supported by a large majority of people. Franco had the support of the army and led an invasion into Spain from Morocco, with the result that civil war raged in Spain for three years. The government forces, who also enlisted supporters and guerrilla fighters from other European countries and Russia, were finally overcome by Franco in 1939. Thousands of loyalists were executed after the war ended in an act of bloody revenge and repression, and Franco remained as dictator until his death in

1975. While in exile, Franco had been denied access to the 'great gulf' of the Mediterranean to prevent him from returning to Spain.

[*Century 9, quatrain 16*]

1937–1945

Romain pouvoir sera du tout à bas,
Son grand voisin imiter ses vestiges;
Occultes haines civiles & debats
Retarderont aux bouffons leurs follies.

Roman power will be completely abased, following the footsteps of his great neighbour. Occult civil hatreds and disputes will delay the folly of these buffoons.

The 'Roman power' referred to in this quatrain is Benito Mussolini, who emulated and copied his 'great neighbour', Adolf Hitler. It is well known that Hitler was fascinated with the occult, and he and other high-ranking members of the Nazi party were slaves to superstition. Hitler and Mussolini could aptly be described as dangerous 'buffoons', given to unpredictable outbursts of rage and other extreme behaviour. Their 'folly' eventually led to their downfall and death.

[*Century 3, quatrain 63*]

1938

L'oyseau de proye volant à la fenestre,
Avant conflit fait aux François parure,
L'un bon prendra, l'autre ambigue sinistre,
La partie foible tiendra par bonne augure.

The bird of prey flying to the window, before conflict with the French, makes preparations. Some will take him as good, others as evil or ambiguous. The weaker party will hold him as a good sign.

The 'bird of prey' is a name given to both Hitler and Napoleon. In this case, the verse fits well with Hitler, as the 'flying to the window' is a good metaphor for Hitler's expansionist aims and his subsequent invasions of Austria, Czechoslovakia and Poland. The split in opinion ('good... evil or ambiguous') could reflect the feelings of Germans early in Hitler's ascendancy, or it may be the division in France between Marshal Pétain, who with his followers fell in with Hitler's authority, and the Vichy cabinet. The 'weaker party' alludes to the growing Nazi Party for whom Hitler became leader and dictator.

[*Century 1, quatrain 34*]

1939

Peuple assemblé voir nouveau spectacle;
Princes & Roys par plusieurs assistans,
Pilliers faillir, murs, mais comme miracle,
Le Roy sauvé & trente des instans.

The people assembled to see a new spectacle, princes and kings with many assistants. The pillars and walls fall, but as if by a miracle the king and thirty others present shall be saved.

This has become known as the 'Krafft Quatrain' because it was used by Ernst Krafft to predict an assassination attempt upon the life of Adolf Hitler. Many high-ranking Nazi leaders were avid believers in astrology and the 'mystical arts' and were familiar with the prophetic quatrains of Nostradamus. Krafft was, in fact, of Swiss nationality, but he was a committed Nazi and was employed as a 'consultant' by Goebbels' Propaganda Ministry. Using the above quatrain and some other calculations, Krafft predicted that an attempt would be made on the Führer's life sometime between 7 and 10 November 1939. He submitted his findings to the Ministry, but since Hitler had forbidden any predictions concerning him to be made it was not acted upon. A mere two days later, Hitler was addressing a large public gathering along with other prominent Nazis. They were called away unexpectedly to Berlin and left earlier than anticipated. Minutes later a bomb, which had been placed behind the rostrum inside a pillar, exploded and killed several of those who were standing nearby. Krafft, instead of earning gratitude for his warning, was suspected of having a hand in the bombing and eventually paid with his life.

[*Century 6, quatrain 51*]

1939–1940

Lors que Serpens viendront à circuir l'air,
Le sang Troyen vexé par les Espagnes,
Par eux, grans nombre en sera faicte rare,
Chef fuit, caché aux mares dans les saignes.

When the snakes shall arrive to surround the air and the French (Trojan) blood is angered by Spain. By them, a great number shall perish. The leader flees and hides in the marshes.

This quatrain is somewhat ambiguous but may refer to the Second World War, when, at the outset, the Germans had superiority in the air. The French had the additional problem of

Spain to deal with. The last part could allude to the fact that the French president and his staff were forced to leave Paris.

The alternative interpretation hinges on 'altar' being used instead of 'air' and on earlier conflicts between France and Spain. This would be towards the end of the sixteenth century (1589–1594). The reference to Trojan blood also implies a link to Catherine de' Medici as the term 'Trojan blood' describes royal French blood, derived, so legend has it, from a mythical son of King Priam of Troy.

[*Century 1, quatrain 19*]

Invasion of France

Freins, Antibol, villes autour de Nice,
Seront vastees fort, par mer & par terre,
Les sauterelles terre & mer vent propice,
Prins, morts, trossez, pillez sans loy de guerre.

Frejus, Antibes, the towns around Nice shall be strongly devastated by land and sea; the locusts by land and sea with the wind favourable, captured, killed, trussed, plundered without the rules of warfare.

France is overcome by land and sea by the ravaging 'locusts' that are Hitler's armies.

[*Century 3, quatrain 80*]

En l'an bien proche eslongné de Venus,
Les deux plus grands de l'Asie & d'Affrique,
Du Rin & Hyster, qu'on dira sont venus,
Cris, pleurs à Malte & costé à Lygustique.

In the year that is soon to come not far from Venus, the two greatest ones of Asia and Africa shall be said to have come from the Rhine and Hitler. Cries and tears at Malta and on the Ligurian shore.

If Venus is taken to mean Venice, then this verse probably describes the alliance between the Italians, Germans and Japanese in the early stages of the Second World War. Hitler and Mussolini met at the Brenner Pass, quite near to Venice, to discuss the Tripartite Pact involving Japan (Asia). The last line alludes to the various operations at this stage of the war.

[*Century 4, quatrain 68*]

Translatera en la grand Germanie,
Brabant & Flandres, Gand, Bruges & Bologne;
La treue sainte le grand duc d'Armenie,
Assaillira Vienne & la Cologne.

He will translate into the Great Germany, Brabant and Flanders, Ghent, Bruges and Boulogne. The truce feigned, the great Duke of Armenia shall assault Vienna and Cologne.

The 'Great Germany' is Hitler and his war machine, which swept across Europe bringing all the places mentioned in the quatrain under the rule of the Third Reich. The 'feigned truce' may be Hitler's allegedly 'defensive' invasion of Poland. Russia is 'the great Duke of Armenia', whose armies penetrated southwards into German territory.

[*Century 5, quatrain 94*]

1939–1945 see 1815

1939–1945

Le gros mastin de cité dechassé,
Sera fasché de l'estrange alliance,
Apres aux champs avoir le chef chassé,
Le Loup & l'ours se donneront defiance.

1939–1945

The great mastiff from the city is driven, being enraged by a strange alliance. After having chased the stag to the field, the wolf and the bear will defy each other.

The great mastiff is interpreted here as meaning the English bulldog and possibly Winston Churchill. Great Britain was angered by the foreign alliances being formed in the pre-war years and eventually, after a period of uncertainty itself entered the Second World War (chased the stag to the battlefield). The wolf may refer to Italy or Germany while the bear is Russia—Britain's ally after the German Wehrmacht attacked the Russian forces.

[*Century 5, quatrain 4*]

Tant d'ans les guerres, en Gaule dureront,
Outre la course du Castulon Monarque,
Victoire incerte trois grands couroneront
Aigle, Coq, Lune, Lyon, Soleil en marque.

For so many years the wars in France will last, beyond the course of the Castilian kings. An uncertain victory shall crown three great ones; the eagle, the cock, the moon, the lion, the sun in its mark.

Wars in France, after the end of the Spanish monarchy ('Castilian kings') would suggest we are dealing with the Second World War. It is by no means unequivocal but three of the Allies are represented: America ('the eagle'); France ('the cock') and Britain ('the lion'). 'The sun in its mark (or house)' could refer either directly to Japan, the Land of the Rising Sun, or to the fact that the final surrender from Japan came in August (in the sun sign Leo).

[*Century 1, quatrain 31*]

De nuict soleil penseront avoir veu,
Quand le pourceau demy homme on verra;
Bruit, chant, bataille au Ciel battre apperceu
Et bestes brutes à parler on orra.

They will think to have seen the sun at night, when they see the hog, half-man. Noise, screams, battles in the sky will be seen, and brute beasts shall be heard to speak.

This quatrain can be interpreted quite readily despite some seemingly surreal qualities. It again refers to war, and specifically to air battles at night. Seeing 'the sun at night' correlates with either the flashes of exploding bombs (and subsequent fires) or the searchlights used by defending forces. The 'hog, half-man' could well be the fighter aeroplane pilot with his helmet, goggles and oxygen mask. The noise and screams would be the sounds of war. Radio equipment is hinted at in the last part, assuming that the 'brute beasts' are the pilots communicating with each other.

[*Century 1, quatrain 64*]

Naples, Palerme, Sicile, Syracuses,
Nouveaux tyrans, fulgures, feux celestes,
Forces de Londres, Gands, Bruxelles & Suses,
Grand hecatombe, triumphe, faire festes.

Naples, Palermo, Sicily, Syracuse, new tyrants, lightning and celestial fires. A force from London, Ghent, Brussels and Susa; a great slaughter then triumph and festivities.

A quatrain alluding to Italy's part in the Second World War. The 'new tyrants' are Mussolini and the Fascists. The lightning and celestial fires are warfare, with Britain and the Allies victorious and rejoicing after much slaughter.

[*Century 2, quatrain 16*]

1939–1945

> *Bestes farouches de faim fleuves tranner,*
> *Plus part du camp encontre Hister sera,*
> *En cage de fer le grand fera trainner,*
> *Quand rien enfant Germain observera.*

Beasts, fierce due to hunger, shall cross rivers, the greater part of the battlefield shall be against Hister. He will drag the great one in a cage of iron, when the child of Germany observes no law.

This remarkable quatrain describes Hitler ('Hister') who is the 'child of Germany' who 'observes no law'. The German advance over Europe in the early years of the Second World War was dependent upon the crossing of bridges, and this is described in the opening line. The iron cage perhaps refers to the subjection of so many peoples. Hitler identified himself in this and some of the other quatrains and attached great significance to prophecy.

[*Century 2, quatrain 24*]

> *Un an devant le conflit Italique,*
> *Germain, Gaulois, Espagnols pour le fort,*
> *Cherra l'escolle maison de republique,*
> *Ou, hors mis peu, seront suffoquez morts.*

One year before the Italian conflict, Germans, French and Spanish shall be for the strong one; the school house of the republic shall fall, where, except for a few, they will suffocate to death.

> *Un peu apres non point longue intervalle,*
> *Par mer & terre sera fait grand tumulte,*
> *Beaucoup plus grande sera pugne navalle,*
> *Feux, animaux, qui plus feront d'insulte.*

A little while afterwards, not a long interval, by sea and land shall a great tumult be raised. The naval battles will be much greater. Fires, beasts shall make more affront.

The opening lines of quatrain 39 allude to the fact that the 'strong one', Hitler, commanded significant support both in Germany and some other European countries before the Second World War. The 'school house of the republic' may refer to France, or, alternatively, Italy. In both countries many people suffered and were killed.

Quatrain 40 appears to be continuation, with the great land and sea battles of the Second World War being referred to. 'Fires' and 'beasts' may indicate firing from submarines and explosions at sea.

[*Century 2, quatrains 39 and 40*]

D'où pensera faire venir famine,
De là viendra le rassasiement;
L'œil de la mer par avare canine,
Pour de l'un l'autre donra huille froment.

From whence one thought to bring famine, from thence shall come satisfaction. The eye of the sea by a canine covetousness for the one and the other will give oil and wheat.

These lines can be attributed to the attempted blockade of Britain by the German navy during the Second World War. Although there were shortages and rationing of food supplies, there was no famine. Some ships got through, bringing in essential supplies, especially from the United States. The 'eye of the sea' with its 'canine covetousness' may refer to the periscope of each German U-boat. The U-boats certainly proved devastating to the Atlantic convoys during the Second World War.

[*Century 4, quatrain 15*]

1940s see 1651

1940

Du tout Marseille des habitans changee
Course & pour fuitte jusques pres de Lyon.
Narbon, Tholoze par Bordeaux outragee,
Tuez, captifs, presque d'un million.

The inhabitants of Marseilles will change completely, running and pursued as far as Lyons. Narbonne, Toulouse, outraged by Bordeaux. The killed and captive will be almost one million.

The naming of French cities in this quatrain and the magnitude of the number of casualties fits well with the Second World War and the Vichy régime of Marshal Pétain. When the German forces moved into Paris in 1940, the French government fled to Bordeaux, while the other cities named fell under the control of the Vichy régime.

The number of casualties mentioned is higher than the 680,000 French dead or wounded, but if the Allies who fought alongside the French are included, then one million is reasonably accurate. The reference to the 'inhabitants of Marseilles' changing is, in all likelihood, the fact that they underwent occupation by the Germans, which certainly resulted in far-reaching changes.

[*Century 1, quatrain 72*]

Les fugitifs feu du ciel sus les piques,
Conflit prochain des corbeaux s'esbatans;
De terre on crie aide secours celiques,
Quand pres des murs seront les combatans.

The fugitive, fire from heaven on to their weapon. The imminent conflict involving the crows. From earth they cry for heavenly help when the combatants shall be near the walls.

This is believed to refer to the fall of France to the invading German armies in 1940. Retreating French soldiers and refugees were forced to flee towards Paris and came under relentless aerial bombardment ('fire from heaven'). Bodies were left where they fell and were prey to carrion crows. The last lines appear to refer to Paris itself in the days before the city fell to the occupying German forces.

[*Century 3, quatrain 7*]

1940 and 1944–1945

Le grand Empire sera tost desolé,
Et translaté pres d'Arduenne silve;
Les deux bastards pres l'aisné decollé,
Et regnera Aeneodarb, nez de milve.

The great empire shall soon be made desolate and altered near the woods of the Ardennes. The two bastards by the oldest will be cut off and Aenodarb shall reign, the one with the nose of hawk.

These lines may be a prediction of events in the Second World War, when France ,'the great empire', was lost to Germany. There were battles in and around the Ardennes region, both in 1940 and 1944–1945. The 'bastards' may be the defeated French generals who failed to halt the German advance. The 'oldest' one could be Maxime Weygand, who took over as commander-in-chief, and the 'hawk-nosed' one General Charles de Gaulle.

[*Century 5, quatrain 45*]

1940–1942

Le vieux frustré du principal espoir,
Il parviendra au chef de son empire;
Vingt mois tiendra le regne à grand pouvoir,
Tiran, cruel en delaissant un pire.

The old man, frustrated in his principal hope, shall attain to the headship of his empire. Twenty months he shall hold the kingdom with great power, a tyrant cruel and giving way to one worse.

The most likely explanation of this quatrain is that it describes the brief period, from 1940 to 1942, when Marshal Pétain headed the government of France. In April 1942, he was forced to surrender any remaining power to the Germans.

[*Century 8, quatrain 65*]

1940–1944

Le changement sera fort difficile,
Cité province au change gain sera,
Cœur haut, prudent mis, chassé luy habile,
Mer, terre, peuple, son estat changera.

The change shall be truly difficult. Both city and province will gain by the change. A man of high, prudent heart shall be chased out by the cunning one. By land and sea people shall change their estate.

This quatrain refers to General Charles de Gaulle, who is the 'high, prudent heart' and who was 'chased out' to exile in London. The change was 'truly difficult' for him, but eventually he became the eminent leader of post-war France. The last lines of the verse presumably refer to the efforts to free France from German occupation and the great changes that this involved for so many people.

[*Century 4, quatrain 21*]

Le vieux mocqué, & privé de sa place,
Par l'estranger qui le subornera;
Mains de son fils mangees devant sa face,
Les freres à Chartres, Orleans, Rouen trahyra.

The old man is mocked and deprived of his place by the foreigner who will suborn him. The hands of his sons are eaten up before his face, he will betray his brother at Chartres, Orléans and Rouen.

This verse describes Marshal Pétain, whose nickname was 'the old man', and his collaboration with the Germans during the Second World War. Pétain negotiated an agreement with Germany, but the terms of this were disregarded by the occupation forces. Pétain was hated by his compatriots and deprived of his position by the Germans. The 'hands of his sons' are his supporters who were swept away along with Pétain. The 'brother' is the Allies, who eventually liberated France. Chartres, Orléans and Rouen were all set free by the Allies on 19 August 1944. Pétain was initially sentenced to death for treason but this was later changed to a life sentence.

[*Century 4, quatrain 61*]

Le Neron jeune dans les trois cheminées,
Fera de paiges vifs pour ardoir jetter,
Heureux qui loing sera de tels menées,
Trois de son sang le feront mort guetter.

The new Nero in three chimneys will make the thrown out living pages to burn. Happy is he who is far from such events, three of his family will seize him to put him to death.

This has been interpreted by some as referring to the Nazi concentration camps and victims being burned in the ovens. The last lines are taken to relate to the attempted assassination of Hitler by Colonel von Stauffenburg and General Beck in 1944. Both conspirators (members of the Nazi 'family') were executed after the attempt failed but perhaps there was a third whose involvement was not discovered.

[*Century 9, quatrain 53*]

1940–1945

Et Ferdinand blonde sera descorte,
Quitter la fleur, suyure le Macedon,
Au grand besoing defaillira sa routte,
Et marchera contre le Myrmiden.

And the blonde Ferdinand will be in disagreement to discard the flower and follow the Macedonian. In great need his route will fail and he will march against the Myrmidons.

This quatrain could refer to the Bulgarian King Ferdinand during the Second World War. The Macedonians may be the Spanish and the other reference may be to the Greeks or Germans.

[*Century 9, quatrain 35*]

Le grand sepulchre du peuple Aquitanique
S'approchera aupres de la Toscane,
Quand Mars sera pres du coing Germanique,
Et au terroir de la gent Mantuane.

The huge sepulchre of the French people will approach from near to Italy, when war is near the German corner and in the territory of the Italian people.

This quatrain seems to describe best the circumstances of the Second World War when Italy and Germany were allies and there was enormous loss of life among the French.

[*Century 3, quatrain 32*]

Ceux dans les Isles de long temps assiegez,
Prendront vigueur force contre ennemis,
Ceux par dehors morts de faim profliegez
En plus grand faim que jamais seront mis.

Those in the islands besieged for a long time, will undertake vigorous measures against their enemies. Those outside, overcome, will die of hunger by such great starvation as has never happened before.

The opening lines of this quatrain apparently refer to the 'islands' of Great Britain, which stood virtually alone against the might of Germany in the early part of the Second World War. The Atlantic convoys (part of the 'vigorous measures' employed by Britain) were subjected to devastating attacks by the German navy, and the country ran short of many necessary supplies with food being strictly rationed. The 'vigorous measures' were effective, and British people did not starve. However, the rest of the quatrain seems to refer to the situation in the rest of continental Europe, where so many people died of hunger as well as from the conflict itself. 'Such great starvation as has never happened before' can be directly linked with the situation in the Nazi concentration camps in which this means of killing people was deliberately used.

[*Century 3, quatrain 71*]

Apres victoire de raibeuse langue,
L'esprit tempté en tranquil & repos;
Victeur sanguin par conflit fait harengue,
Rostir la langue & la chair & les os.

1940–1945

After the victory of the raging tongue, the spirit in tranquillity and rest. The bloody victor harangues throughout the conflict, roasting the tongue, the flesh and the bones.

This quatrain describes Adolf Hitler, whose hallmark was his raging speeches. The final line is a grim reference to the ovens of the concentration camps.

[*Century 4, quatrain 56*]

Par les Sueves & lieux circonvoisins,
Seront en guerres pour cause des nuees,
Gamp marins locustes & cousins,
Du Leman fautes seront bien desnuees.

Through the Swiss (Switzerland) and the surrounding areas, they will resort to war because of the clouds, the sea, locusts and gnats, the faults of Geneva shall appear very naked.

The failure of the League of Nations and the outbreak of the Second World War are predicted in this quatrain.

[*Century 5, quatrain 85*]

Norneigre & Dace, & l'isle Britanique,
Par les unis freres seront vexees;
Le chef Romain issu du sang Gallique,
Et les copies aux forests repoulsees.

Norway and Dacia and the British island, will be vexed by the united brothers. The Roman chief issued from French blood, and the forces repulsed into the forests.

The 'united brothers' may be Hitler and Mussolini, who so 'vexed' other nations during the Second World War. The 'forces repulsed into the forests' may be the network of the French Resistance who continually troubled Germany and helped to bring about that country's eventual downfall.

[*Century 6, quatrain 7*]

> *Par fraude, regne, forces expolier,*
> *La classe obsesse, passages à l'espie;*
> *Deux faincts amis se viendront t'allier,*
> *Esueiller haine de long temps assoupie.*

By the kingdom an army despoiled, the fleet possessed, passages for spies. Two false friends shall agree to rally together; they shall raise up a hatred that has been dormant for a long time.

> *En grand regret sera la gent Gauloise,*
> *Cœur vain, leger croira temerité;*
> *Pain, sel, ne vin, eau, venin ne cervoise,*
> *Plus grand captif, faim, froid, necessité.*

The French nation shall be in great regret, their heart vain and light shall believe rashly. No bread, salt, wine, water, venom or ale shall they have, the greater part of them shall be captives, hungry, cold and in want.

Both these quatrains can be applied to events in the Second World War. In the first, the alliance between Hitler and Mussolini (the 'two false friends' who 'agree to rally together') is described, along with the hatred of war and aggression. The second verse relates to the occupation of France and the hardship and suffering of so many people, especially those who were sent to concentration camps.

[*Century 7, quatrains 33 and 34*]

1941

> *La tour de Boucq craindra fuste Barbare*
> *Un temps, long temps apres barque hesperique,*
> *Bestial, gens, meubles tous deux feront grand tare*
> *Taurus & Libra quelle mortelle picque.*

1941

The Tower of Bouk (taken as Tobruk) will be in awe of the barbarian fleet, for a while, a long time after the Spanish boat. Cattle, people, all will be greatly damaged. Taurus and Libra, what a deadly dispute.

The interpretation of this quatrain clearly depends upon the place name, Tobruk. It may be that the Tower of Bouk (*Tour de Boucq* in the original) was the nearest equivalent at that time for Tobruk. This being so, it would seem to refer to the invasion in 1941, although the 'Spanish boat' (*hesperique* in the original) has to be loosely translated as 'Western', since the British led the invasion. The conflict was between the British and the Italians. The reference to Taurus and Libra matches reasonably well with the commencement of the siege of Tobruk and its relief (April and October, although the actual relief was in November).

One should perhaps bear in mind, however, that there is a Tower of Bouk at the mouth of the River Rhône, and this quatrain may therefore be less significant than at first appears.

[*Century 1, quatrain 28*]

Navalle pugne nuict sera superee,
Le feu, aux naves a l'occident ruine;
Rubriche neuve, la grand nef coloree,
Ire a vaincu, & victoire en bruine.

In a sea fight night will be overcome, the fire, in the ships of the West, ruined. A new stratagem, the great coloured ship, anger to the defeated and victory in a mist.

Much of this quatrain fits very well with the incident at Pearl Harbor during the Second World War. Japanese planes made an early morning attack on the American Pacific fleet, which had recently moved from its base in California to Pearl Harbor in Hawaii. The attack happened on Sunday 7 December, and by 9.30 am tremendous damage had been wrought. Of course, this event ensured that the United States joined the Allied forces in the war. The 'new stratagem' could refer to the type of attack instigated at Pearl Harbor and the 'coloured ship' could well be the camouflage adopted during times of war. Although 'anger to the defeated' has been taken to mean Japan, it could equally be the anger felt by all of America, which precipitated them into war, with victory coming to them and the Allies, albeit through a mist of time and war.

[*Century 9, quatrain 100*]

1942

Entre Gaulois le dernier honoré,
D'homme ennemy sera victorieux,
Force & terroir en moment exploré,
D'un coup de trait quand mourra l'envieux.

The man that is least honoured among the French shall be victorious over the man who was his enemy. Strength and lands shall in a while be explored when suddenly the envious one dies from the shot.

The opening lines are usually said to describe General Charles de Gaulle and the eventual triumph of France over the 'enemy', Hitler. The man who was assassinated was Admiral Darlan, who met his death on Christmas Eve 1942.

[*Century 3, quatrain 100*]

1944–1945 or 2005

L'an ensuyvant descouverts par deluge,
Deux chefs esleuz, le premier ne tiendra,
De fuyr ombre à l'un d'eux le refuge,
Saccagée case qui premier maintiendra.

1945

The year following discovered by a deluge, two chiefs elected, the first shall not hold on; of fleeing shadows to one shall be a refuge; the victim plundered who maintained the first.

This verse is thought, by some commentators, to be a reference to Mussolini and his flight into Germany after losing power. He found refuge for a while but soon both Hitler and Mussolini were destroyed.

[*Century 9, quatrain 4*]

1945

Aupres des portes & dedans deux citez,
Seront deux fleaux onc n'apperceu un tel,
Faim dedans peste, de fer hors gens boutez,
Crier secours au grand Dieu immortel.

Near the harbours and in two cities will be two scourges, the like of which have never been seen. Famine, plague within, people thrust out by the sword will cry for help to the great God immortal.

This quatrain refers to the dropping of the atomic bombs by the United States on Hiroshima and Nagasaki. These were both coastal cities, and destruction on such a scale and of this horrific nature had never been seen before. Over 100,000 people were killed or incinerated, and of those that survived many died in agony in the following days. They succumbed to hunger, thirst and radiation sickness and lacked medical aid, resembling the plague victims familiar to Nostradamus. The scale of their suffering is reflected in the last two lines of the quatrain.

[*Century 2, quatrain 6*]

1945

> *Ruyné aux Volsques de peur si fort terribles,*
> *Leur grand cité taincte, faict pestilent;*
> *Piller Sol, Lune, & violer leurs temples;*
> *Et les deux fleuves rougir de sang coulant.*

Ruin shall come to the vandals of a fear so very terrible; their great city shall be tainted by a pestilential deed. They shall plunder sun and moon and violate their temples, and the two rivers shall run red with blood.

This quatrain accurately describes the terrible destruction of the Japanese city of Hiroshima by a nuclear bomb dropped by the United States in August 1945. There was enormous loss of life, both as a direct result of the bombing and in the days, months and years that followed. The city was virtually flattened, and fires raged, blackening the sky. Hiroshima is situated between two rivers; many of the initial survivors, who were horribly burned, crawled to the water and died there. The city was indeed 'tainted' by pestilence since that day in the effects of radiation sickness and genetic abnormalities that have beset the people. A similar fate befell the city of Nagasaki.

[*Century 6, quatrain 98*]

> *La grand cite d'Occean maritime,*
> *Environnée de marets en cristal;*
> *Dans le solstice hyemal & la prime,*
> *Sera tentée de vent espouvental.*

The great maritime city of the ocean, encompassed by a crystal swamp. In the solstice of winter and in the spring, will be tried by a wind very dreadful.

This quatrain has been interpreted as a further reference to the fearful destruction of Hiroshima and Nagasaki.

[*Century 9, quatrain 48*]

1945

> *Trente adherans de l'ordre des quirettes*
> *Bannis, leurs biens donnez ses adversaires,*
> *Tous leurs bienfaits seront pour demerites*
> *Classe espargie delivrez aux corsaires.*

Thirty adherents of the order of the Quirites, banished, their goods given to their adversaries. All their good deeds will be accounted to their discredit, the fleet scattered, they shall be delivered to the Corsairs.

If the Corsairs are the Russians, then this can be applied to the situation in post-war Italy after the fall of the Fascists.

[*Century 10, quatrain 77*]

Hitler's bunker

> *Les forteresses des assiegez ferrez,*
> *Par poudre à feu profondes en abysme;*
> *Les pr600diteurs seront tous vifs serrez,*
> *Onc aux Sacrifices n'advint si piteux scisme.*

The fortress of the besieged shall be hard-pressed, by gunpowder sunk into a pit; the traitors will be shut up alive, never did such a pitiful schism rend the sextons (Saxons or Germans).

If the use of the word 'sextons' by Nostradamus is interpreted as referring to the Saxons or Germans, then this quatrain could apply to the last remnant loyal to Hitler, shut up in the bunker in Berlin as the Allies approached in the closing stages of the Second World War.

[*Century 4, quatrain 40*]

1952 see **1837–1901**

1956

Par vie & mort changé regne d'Hongrie,
La loy sera plus aspre que service;
Leur grand cité d'urlemens, plaints & cris,
Castor & Pollux ennemis dans la lice.

By life and death the reign in Hungary shall be changed, the law shall become more austere than service. Their great city howls with moans and cries. Castor and Pollux are enemies in the field.

This quatrain seems clearly to foretell the 1956 Hungarian uprising, when the people of Hungary tried to free themselves from domination by the Soviets. The Hungarian premier, Imre Nagy, renounced the Warsaw Pact on 1 November 1956, and the people of Budapest celebrated. However, within three days, Russian tanks had advanced into the country and occupied Budapest, quashing the uprising. The city was damaged, and many Hungarian people, including Premier Nagy, were either killed in the fighting or in the executions that followed. The Soviet régime imposed a harsh, repressive order with very little individual freedom allowed. The reference to the Roman twins, Castor and Pollux, seems to allude to the fact that pro-Russian Hungarians fought against those in favour of the uprising at this time.

[*Century 2, quatrain 90*]

1960–2005

En ce temps là sera frustré Cypres,
De son secours de ceux de mer Egee,
Vieux trucidez, mais par Masles & Liphres,
Seduict leur Roy, Royne plus outragee.

1963

At that time Cyprus shall be frustrated of its aid from those of the Aegean sea; old ones shall be killed but by arms and supplications, the king shall be seduced and the queen more outraged.

This quatrain appears to quite neatly describe the long-lasting political situation in the divided island of Cyprus, which endless negotiations for more than 40 years have failed to resolve. The king and queen referred to here may represent political leaders and movements. In a recent referendum, the majority Greek population in the south of the island voted against re-unification—an extremely unpopular decision in Europe and internationally. However, the minority Turkish population in the north voted overwhelmingly in favour—a sign of the great shift in opinion that there has been among Turkey's government and people on the status of the so-called 'Turkish Republic of Northern Cyprus'. This shift has been brought about, to a large extent, by Turkey's desire to become a member of the European Union but somewhat bizarrely, it is the intransigent Greek south of Cyprus which is now a member while the Turkish north still remains excluded.

[*Century 3, quatrain 89*]

1963

La mort subiette du premier personnage,
Aura changé & mis un autre au regne,
Tost, tard venu a si haut & bas aage,
Que terre & mer faudra qu'on le craingne.

The sudden death of the premier personage will bring about change, cause another to rule. Soon, but too late came he to high office, by land and sea it will be necessary to fear him.

The whole quatrain seems to apply quite well to American President John F. Kennedy, who was assassinated in 1963. He was a young president who due to his early demise, was not able to fulfil the expectations held by many in his own country and abroad. In 1961, he attempted to invade Cuba—and was feared 'by land and sea'—but the whole affair was a fiasco for which the USA was criticised. However, Kennedy was also a reformer and held issues of social and racial justice close to his heart and was held in affection and high regard by most Americans.

[*Century 4, quatrain 14*]

Le grand du fondre tombe d'heure diurne,
Mal & predit par porteur postulaire,
Suyvant presage tombe d'heure nocturne
Conflit, Reims, Londres, Etrusque pestifere.

The great man shall fall in daylight, struck by a thunderbolt, an evil event predicted by the bearer of a petition. According to the prediction another one falls at the hour of night. There is conflict in Reims, London and pestilence in Tuscany.

Most commentators place this quatrain as a prediction of the assassination of the two Kennedy brothers. President John F. Kennedy was shot in broad daylight in Dallas, Texas on 22 November 1963, while being driven through the streets in an open-topped limousine in front of a cheering crowd. His killer was Lee Harvey Oswald. Many threats had been made against the president's life and only a week beforehand, a psychic, Jeanne Dixon, had advised the cancellation of the visit to Dallas. Five years later in California, 'another one'—Robert Kennedy, President Kennedy's brother—was celebrating his victory in the presidential primary elections when he too was gunned down at 1 am on the morning of 5 June 1968. Once again, Jeanne Dixon had apparently tried to warn the presidential candidate of the potential danger in which he stood. There was international consternation after both these assassinations, and the summer of 1968 is also remembered for the student demonstrations that took place in Paris and London during that year.

[*Century 1, quatrain 26*]

1963

> *Devant le peuple sang sera respandu,*
> *Que du haut ciel ne viendra eslongner;*
> *Mais d'un long-temps ne sera entendu,*
> *L'esprit d'un seul le viendra tesmoigner.*

Before the people blood will be spilt, which from the high heavens will not go far. But for a long time it shall not be heeded, the spirit of one shall come to witness it.

President John F. Kennedy's assassination in 1963 was witnessed not only by the crowd lining the streets of Dallas but by television viewers throughout the world, who indeed saw 'the blood spilt'. Conspiracy theories abounded after the event and many disbelieved the official view that the president had been shot from a high window in a nearby building by Lee Harvey Oswald. Some resolutely believed that the fatal shot had been fired by an unknown assassin from a low, grassy mound near the road and the blurred photograph of a man standing there was later produced as supporting evidence.

[*Century 4, quatrain 49*]

> *Le successeur vengera son beau frere,*
> *Occuper regne souz ombre de vengeance,*
> *Occis ostacle son sang mort vitupere,*
> *Long temps Bretagne tiendra avec la France.*

The successor will avenge his handsome brother and will occupy the realm under the shade of vengeance, the obstacle of the blameworthy dead has been killed, for a long time shall Britain hold with France.

This quatrain could possibly apply to Robert Kennedy who

seemed set to become president, after the untimely death of his good-looking brother John—a shadow that hung over America for a long time. Blame for President John F. Kennedy's assassination was of course heaped upon Lee Harvey Oswald. The last line, describing the alliance between Britain and France does not seem to be particularly appropriate.

[*Century 10, quatrain 26*]

1967

Nouvelle loy terre neuve occuper,
Vers la Syrie, Judee, & Palestine,
Le grand Empire Barbare corruer,
Avant que Phebe son siecle determine.

A new law shall occupy a new land towards Syria, Judea and Palestine. The great Barbarian empire will fall down before the century of Phoebe is determined.

The opening lines of this quatrain refer to establishment of the state of Israel, and also the Six Days' War between 5 and 10 June 1967. The 'great Barbarian empire' means the Arab countries that lost so much of their land to the Israelis. There was considerable loss of life, and many people became refugees, forced into a permanent existence in camps a long way from home. Israel occupied the 'new land' of the Golan Heights, Gaza Strip, West Bank and South Lebanon, and there has been continual conflict ever since in spite of great efforts to reach a peaceful, just settlement. The implication is that the eventual outcome will favour Israel.

[*Century 3, quatrain 97*]

1970

Dedans le coing de Luna viendra rendre,
Où sera prins & mis en terre estrange,
Les fruicts immeurs seront à grand esclandre,
Grand vitupere, à l'un grande loüange.

He shall come, to return, to the corner of Luna, where he will be taken and put on strange ground. The unripe fruits will be a great scene, a great vilification, to the other great praise.

This would seem to be one of Nostradamus' more remarkable predictions. If 'Luna' is taken, quite reasonably, to mean the moon, then it becomes apparent that man's landing on the moon is the event in question. Clearly the moon would be 'strange ground' (foreign land) to anyone walking on it. However, this is not the first lunar landing, which was Apollo 11 in 1969, but a later mission, Apollo 13. The 'unripe fruits will be a great scene' could therefore be a reference to the technical problems encountered with Apollo 13, resulting in blame but also praise that the astronauts were returned safely, following an explosion in the service module.

[*Century 9, quatrain 65*]

1972

Au revolu du grand nombre septiesme,
Apparoistra au temps ieux d'Hecatombe,
Non esloigné du grand age milliesme,
Que les entrez sortiront de leur tombe.

The year of the great seventh number having revolved, it will appear at the time of the Games of sacrifice, not far from the great age of the millennium, when the buried will emerge from their tombs.

Although this is not particularly clear, the terrible events at the Munich Olympic Games in 1972 do fit with this quatrain. The games were marred by violence and an act of terrorism which sadly became a foretaste of future events that were to become all too common in the following decades. The Olympics had entered their final week when eight Arab terrorists broke into the quarters housing the Israeli athletes, killing two outright and taking a further nine people as hostages. Eventually, a bus was procured to take terrorists and hostages to a military airport, supposedly to board a flight out of the country. But at the airport, the security services attempted a rescue mission and in the ensuing gun battle, all nine of the hostages were killed along with five of the terrorists and one policeman. The Games could justifiably be said to have taken place close to the time of the millennium. Could the buried emerging from their tombs be a possible reference to the mass graves that have been discovered in several parts of the world, notably the former Yugoslavia, Rwanda and Iraq?

[*Century 10, quatrain 74*]

1974

Le grand Senat decernera la pompe,
A un qu'apres sera vaincu, chassé;
Des adherans seront à son de trompe,
Biens publiez, ennemy dechassé.

The great Senate will award the pomp, to one who afterwards will be vanquished, expelled. His adherents will be there at the sound of a trumpet, publicly sold, the enemies driven out.

1979

This quatrain could be applied to anyone who after political success fell short of expectations and was removed or forced out of office. The most obvious subject is American president, Richard Nixon. Following the Watergate Scandal, Nixon resigned in 1974 when threatened with impeachment. The last two lines probably reflect that such events attract a lot of interest and many gained from the event ('publicly sold' could refer to individuals who wrote books, etc, in the wake of Watergate). The last part ('the enemies driven out') may reflect that Nixon became accepted again, almost in the role of an elder statesman, and had therefore driven away his enemies.

[*Century 10, quatrain 76*]

1979 see also 2001

Pluye, faim, guerre, en Perse non cessee,
La foy trop grande trahyra le Monarque,
Par la finie en Gaule commencee,
Secret augure pour à un estre parque.

Rain, famine, war, having not ceased in Persia; too great a trust shall betray the monarch. There it ended, in France it began, a secret sign to one that he shall die.

This quatrain seems reasonably clear in its explanation and can be linked quite readily with the removal of the Shah of Iran (formerly Persia) and the return from exile of the Ayatollah Khomeini, the Iranian religious and political leader. The Shah's reign from 1953 was marked by a gradual increase in social reform and westernization. However, this alienated the more fundamental Islamic groups, and it became necessary to suppress objections and a one-party regime was introduced in 1975. In time the anti-Shah feeling grew, and he was eventually only kept in power by Western interests. The reference to France can be linked with the Ayatollah Khomeini, who was exiled in Paris, from where he orchestrated his campaign against the Shah. Eventually the Shah was forced to leave the country in January 1979, whereupon the Ayatollah Khomeini returned a few days later.

[*Century 1, quatrain 70*]

1979–1989

De l'aquatique triplicité naistra,
D'un qui fera le Jeudy pour sa feste;
Son bruit, los, regne, sa puissance croistra,
Par terre & mer, aux Orients tempeste.

From the aquatic triplicity shall be born one who has Thursday as his holiday. His fame, praise, rule and power will grow, by land and sea, trouble to the east.

There is an interesting astrological aspect to this quatrain, as is often found with the predictions of Nostradamus. There is also some ambiguity. The 'aquatic triplicity' may well refer to someone who has the three water signs of Cancer, Scorpio and Pisces dominant in his astrological chart. Since Thursday is 'his holiday', he is presumably not of the Christian faith, and the Eastern parameter might suggest someone such as the Ayatollah Khomeini.

An alternative might refer to the founding of the United States of America. The 'aquatic triplicity' in this case would then be the three bodies of water around the USA—the Pacific, the Atlantic and the Gulf of Mexico. The holiday on a Thursday would then refer to Thanksgiving Day.

[*Century 1, quatrain 50*]

1981 see 1799

1986

D'humain troupeau neuf seront mis à part,
De jugement & conseil separees,
Leur sort sera divisé en depart,
Cap, Thita, Lambda morts, bannis, esgarez.

Nine shall be detached from the rest of humanity, separated from judgment and counsel. Their fate is to be divided from the time of their departure. Kappa, Theta, Lambda dead, banished and scattered.

Apart from getting the number wrong, Nostradamus could well be predicting here the fate of the crew of the 25th Challenger spacecraft. The destiny of the seven crew members was indeed sealed from the moment of take-off, when they were 'detached' from the rest of the human race and when no intervention or 'counsel' could save them. Up until that moment, on 28 January 1986, the Challenger missions had been a great success for the USA and space travel had almost begun to be regarded as a matter of routine. All pre-flight planning and checks had apparently run smoothly but to the horror of the watching world, in the first minute after take off, the space craft exploded and became a ball of fire killing all those on board. This disaster had a huge effect upon both public and government opinion regarding the sending astronauts into space. Despite more recent successes, America's programme of manned space missions has never fully recovered from the disastrous events of that day, which shocked the world's people out of any sense of complacency regarding mankind's ability to conquer the universe.

[*Century 1, quatrain 81*]

1989

L'oyseau Royal sur la Cité solaire,
Sept mois devant fera nocturne augure;
Mur d'Orient cherra tonnerre esclaire,
Sept jours aux portes les ennemis à l'heure.

The royal bird above the city of the sun, for seven months will give a nightly warning; the wall in the east will fall amid thunder and lightening, in seven days the enemies are at the gates.

The first lines are obscure and seem to be referring to a bird—probably an eagle—giving a warning over Paris or Rome. The 'wall in the east' that falls has been associated with several events in the twentieth century. But perhaps the most dramatic and relevant was the tearing down of the Berlin Wall by jubilant crowds in November 1989—for many, the ultimate symbol of the collapse of communism in Eastern Europe. The final line reminds us that this collapse did not occur without strife—the war in the Balkans and other ongoing conflicts in eastern Europe were foreseen and anticipated.

[*Century 5, quatrain 81*]

Downfall of Nicolae Ceausescu

Quand la Corneille sur tour de brique iointe,
Durant sept heures ne fera que crier,
Mort presagee de sang statuë tainte,
Tyran meurtry aux Dieux peuple prier.

When the crow on the brick tower shall for seven hours do nothing but croak, death is foretold and the statue stained with blood. The tyrant murdered, to their gods the people pray.

The crow is a familiar omen of death in the folklore of many northern countries and here it is said to croak for seven hours from its perch on the top of a tower made of brick. Nicolae Ceaucescu, the ruthless communist dictator and leader of Romania until 1989, violently suppressed all dissent, destroyed much of his country's heritage and enriched himself while many of his people starved. Like many other dictators, he encouraged a cult of personality to develop around his person and this included the erection of many statues of himself and the building of grandiose palaces where no expense was spared. His downfall came as the cracks began to appear in communist regimes throughout Eastern Europe, and in 1989 he and his equally hated wife were summarily executed by their fellow countrymen, although whether a crow called to announce the event is not recorded. Romania now faces a much brighter future as a member state of the European Union.

[*Century 4, quatrain 55*]

1999

L'an mil neuf cens nonante neuf sept mois,
Du ciel viendra un grand Roy d'effrayeur,
Resusciter le grand Roy d'Angolmois,
Avant apres Mars regner par bon heur.

In the year 1999 and seven months, from the sky will come a great, frightening king. To raise again the great King of the Mongols. Before, after, Mars shall reign happily.

Nostradamus is quite specific with his date in this quatrain, and he is predicting doom and gloom for the end of the millennium. Not only does he foretell the appearance of the 'King of the Mongols' (who could be taken to be the third

Antichrist, of Eastern origin) but he also predicts that wars will rage ('Mars shall reign happily') both before and after this period.

[*Century 10, quatrain 72*]

20th century–21st century

Par deux fois haut, par deux fois mis à bas,
L'orient aussi l'occident foiblira,
Son adversaire apres plusieurs combats,
Par mer chassé au besoing faillira.

Twice raised up and twice thrown down, the East will also weaken the West, its adversary after several combats, chased by sea, it will fail at need.

This appears to refer to two attacks by the East upon the West. Could it refer to the terrorist attacks in New York and upon Westerners in several other countries? It seems to say that there will be several conflicts—and already we have seen war in Afghanistan and Iraq—and that defeat will ultimately come to the East by means of a sea battle.

[*Century 8, quatrain 59*]

Faux à l'Estang, joint vers le Sagittaire,
En son haut auge de l'exaltation,
Peste, famine, mort de main militaire,
Le Siecle approcher de renovation.

When a scythe (Saturn) is with a water sign and Sagittarius is exalted on high, plague, famine, death by military hands; the century approaches its renewal.

Most commentators have interpreted this quatrain as predicting a world war at the end of the twentieth century. Although the astrological references are not entirely clear, there has certainly been plague (AIDS), famine (in Africa) and death in too many wars towards the start of the twenty-first century.

[*Century 1, quatrain 16*]

Nuclear weapons in Scotland

Le chef de Londres par regne l'Americh,
L'isle d'Escosse t'empiera par gelée;
Roy Reb auront un si faux Antechrist,
Que les mettra trestous dans la meslée.

The chief of London by American rule, will temper the island of Scotland with a very great cold. Reb the king shall have a false Antichrist, who will put them all into discord.

This has been interpreted as referring to the siting of Polaris and Trident nuclear weapons in Scotland, in accordance with the wishes of America and put into place by the Prime Minister in London. Significant numbers of people in Scotland are opposed both to the presence of nuclear weapons in the country and/or parliamentary rule from Westminster. In the closing lines, Nostradamus once again predicts the coming of an Antichrist—a powerful figure who will throw the nations into discord.

[*Century 10, quatrain 66*]

Occupation of white-owned farms in Zimbabwe

Nouveaux venus, lieu basty sans deffence,
Occuper place par lors inhabitable,
Prez, maisons, champs, villes prendre à plaisance,
Faim, peste, guerre, arpen long labourable.

Newcomers will build a place without defence, occupying places that were previously not habitable. Then meadows, houses, fields, towns will be taken at pleasure. Famine, plague, war, long arable lands.

This quatrain fits Zimbabwe's recent history quite neatly, the first lines describing the newcomers (white people) occupying land and turning it into prosperous farms—something that was not necessarily welcomed by the country's own inhabitants. In recent years and with government sanction, the white farm lands have been seized, very often violently. Many of the people of this once prosperous country are now short of food while the farmland, the 'long, arable lands', remains largely uncultivated.

[*Century 2, quatrain 19*]

> *Les lieux peuplez seront inhabitables,*
> *Pour champs avoir grande division;*
> *Regnes livrez à prudens incapables,*
> *Entre les freres mort & dissention.*

The populated lands shall become uninhabitable, great disagreements in order to obtain fields; lands given to those incapable of prudence, and for the great brothers, death and dissension.

Once again, this seems to be a very apt description of the recent policy of land seizures in Zimbabwe although the identity of the two great brothers is not clear.

[*Century 2, quatrain 95*]

2001

Editor's Note: On 11 September 2001, two passenger planes hijacked by al-Qaeda terrorists deliberately crashed into, and

2001

ultimately destroyed, the World Trade Center in New York, killing thousands of people. It was not long after this event that hoax rumours and urban myths began to circulate, primarily by email. Some claimed that the attack had been predicted by all kinds of sources. Nostradamus was one of these sources. The hoax texts were hybrids of several Nostradamus quatrains and were circulated at a time when people were looking vainly for answers. The following verses are genuine Nostradamus quatrains.

> *Cinq & quarante degrez ciel bruslera,*
> *Feu approcher de la grand cité neuve,*
> *Instant grand flamme esparse sautera,*
> *Quand on voudra des Normans faire preuve.*

Forty-five degrees the sky will burn. Fire engulfs the great new city. Immediately huge scattered flames will shoot upwards, when they wish to see the Normans proven.

Most interpreters agree that the city mentioned here is New York as it lies between the 40th and 45th parallels and previously this quatrain has been interpreted as a nuclear attack. The mention of Normans in the last line has indicated to some interpreters that the quatrain refers to an attack against Paris.

[*Century 6, quatrain 97*]

> *Jardin du monde aupres de cité neufue,*
> *Dans le chemin des montagnes cavées,*
> *Sera saisi & plongé dans la cuve,*
> *Beuvant par force eaux soulphre envenimées.*

Garden of the world, near the new city, in the road of the man-made (or hollow) mountains, it will be seized and plunged into the tank, being forced to drink water inflamed with sulphur.

The 'road of the man-made mountains' seems to indicate skyscrapers. The 'new city' is taken to be New York. Other interpreters have suggested the 'garden of the world' as being Harrisburg in Pennsylvania where there was a nuclear reactor meltdown at Three Mile Island. The sulphur could be the potential contamination of the water supply with radioactive material. The middle section ('seized and plunged into the tank') could be the physical meltdown of the core.

[*Century 10, quatrain 49*]

Par gent estrange, & de Romains loingtaine,
Leur grand cité apres eau fort troublee;
Fille sans main, trop different domaine,
Prins, chef terreure n'avoit este riblee.

By a foreign people and a remote nation, the great city near the water shall be much troubled. A girl without a greatly different estate will be taken, the iron not having been pillaged.

This quatrain has been ascribed to the attack by the Japanese on Pearl Harbour in 1941, but it could also be applied to the destruction of the Twin Towers in New York, although the final lines do not seem to be relevant.

[*Century 2, quatrain 54*]

Soleil levant un grand feu on verra,
Bruit & clarté vers Aquilon tendant;
Dedans le rond mort & cris on orra,
Par glaive, feu, faim, mort les attendans.

At the sun's rising, a great fire shall be seen, noise and light tending towards the north; Within the round globe death and cries are heard, by weapons, fire and famine, death awaits them.

A devastating attack will take place in the north at sunrise, causing death and destruction on a wide scale. Some will die in the attack and others in the fires that take hold afterwards and their voices will be heard crying out. It is very tempting indeed to connect this with the terrible attacks in America in 2001 where such events did indeed take place (although not at sunrise) and the only other detail that appears to be wrong is the prediction of death as a result of famine.

[*Century 2, quatrain 91*]

Osama bin Laden

Par toute Asie grande proscription,
Mesme en Mysie, Lysie, & Pamphylie;
Sang versera par absolution,
D'un jeune noir remply de felonnie.

Through the whole of Asia there shall be a great proscription, the same as in Mysia, Lycia and Pamphilia. Blood shall be spilled by absolution of a young, dark man filled with evil intent.

The places referred to are in the Middle East and Asia and this quatrain seems to imply that many will sign up to the leader's cause—a leader who could be Osama bin Laden and the 'many' followers of Al Qaeda.

[*Century 3, quatrain 60*]

Une nouvelle secte de Philosophes,
Mesprisant mort, or, honneurs & richesses,
Des monts Germains ne seront limitrophes,
A les ensuyure auront appuy & presses.

A new sect of philosophers shall arise; they shall despise death, gold, honours and riches. They shall not be limited by the mountains of Germany, in their following there will be crowds of support.

This quatrain could be applied to any group of fanatical extremists whose minds are wholly bent on their cause. It would seem a fairly fitting description of the fanatical Islamic militant sects and the suicide bombers who are currently wreaking so much havoc in the world.

[*Century 3, quatrain 67*]

Modern communications

Quand l'animal à l'homme domestique
Apres grand peine & sauts viendra parler;
Le foudre à vierge sera si malefique,
De terre prinse & suspenduë en l'air.

When the animal domesticated by man begins to speak after great labour and leaping, the lightening so hurtful to the rod shall be taken from the ground and suspended in the air.

This has been interpreted as referring to modern radio or television communication but equally could apply to mobile phones and their masts. If this is so, the 'animal' referred to is the technology involved.

[*Century 3, quatrain 44*]

2003

Ceux qui auront entrepris subvertir,
Nompareil regne puissant & invincible,
Feront par fraude, nuicts trois advertir,
Quand le plus grand à table lira Bible.

2003

Those who will have an enterprise to subvert an unparalleled kingdom, powerful and invincible. They will deceive, warn of three nights when the greatest one is at his table, reading the Bible.

Given the background surrounding the recent war in Iraq, it is tempting to ascribe this quatrain to these events. To the vast majority of the Iraqi people, it must have seemed that Saddam Hussein was powerful and invincible and that their subjugation was complete and virtually unparalleled in the modern world. Many now believe that the Allies, particularly the USA and Great Britain, went to war on the basis of false intelligence and an exaggeration of the threat posed by Iraq. There were many warnings and nights of anticipation and anxiety before the outbreak of war and it is well known that both President George Bush and Prime Minister Tony Blair rely heavily upon their Christian faith and reading of the Bible.

[*Century 5, quatrain 83*]

Alliance between the USA and the UK

Le regne à deux laissé bien peu tiendront,
Trois ans sept mois passez feront la guerre;
Les deux vestales contre rebelleront,
Victor puis nay en Armonique terre.

The reign is left to two who hold it for a very short time; three years and seven months having passed they will go to war. The two vestals (? vassals) will stage a rebellion against them, the victor will be born in the American land.

This could be attributed to the 'special relationship' between the USA and Great Britain and the decision to engage in the hugely controversial war in Iraq. In both countries, the period of political leadership is generally brief. The two vassal states could be Afghanistan and Iraq where insurgent violence has been unrelenting in the face of what is perceived to be unjust, foreign occupation. But here, Nostradamus is clear about who the victor will be.

[*Century 4, quatrain 95*]

Iraq War or *Events in the Second World War*

De feu volant la machination,
Viendra troubler au grand chef assiegez;
Dedans sera telle sedition,
Qu'en desespoir seront les profligez.

The flying fire machine will come to trouble the great, besieged chief. Within there will be such sedition that the abandoned ones will be in a state of despair.

This quatrain could apply to the aerial bombardment of many cities during the Second World War or more recently, to the war in Iraq. It accurately portrays the terrible state of helplessness, despair and suffering that civilians endure during a time of war.

[*Century 6, quatrain 34*]

2004

A l'ennemy, l'ennemy foy promise,
Ne se tiendra, les captifs retenus;
Prins preme mort, & le reste en chemise,
Donnant le reste pour estre secourus.

To the enemy, the enemy faith promised will not be held, the captives retained; the first is taken, close to death and the rest in their underclothes, damned are the rest for being sustainers.

2004

This quatrain describes a situation where people have been taken hostage and have been forced to take off some of their clothing. In Iraq, some hostages taken by extreme, militant groups have been displayed wearing orange suits and many have been executed. In Beslan Number One School in the republic of North Ossetia, Russia, more than 1,000 hostages were taken by Chechen terrorist separatists on 1 September 2004. The siege continued for three days in the eye of the world's media. Some of the hostages managed to get out and few will forget the dreadful sight of little children running, dressed only in their underwear. The siege ended violently when the building was stormed by soldiers and tragically, over 300 people were killed, many of them children. Of the rest, several hundred were injured and it will take many years for the physical and emotional scars of this ordeal to heal.

Afterwards, the true extent of the suffering of the hostages was revealed. The conditions inside the school were unbearable—very hot and with no access to drinking water. The children stripped down to their underclothes in an attempt to stay cool. Their captors kept them in a state of great physical distress and fear.

[*Century 10, quatrain 1*]

The Asian tsunami or Election of President George Bush to second term in office

L'an ensuyvant descouverts par deluge,
Deux chefs esleuz, le premier ne tiendra,
De fuyr ombre à l'un d'eux le refuge,
Saccagée case qui premier maintiendra.

The year after is discovered by a deluge, two leaders are elected, the first one will not hold on; for one of the two, refuge in fleeing shades, the victim of the hunt plundered who maintained the first.

This is not an easy quatrain to decipher but it could possibly be applied to the election of George Bush (who cannot hold office beyond a second term) and the terrible flooding caused by the tsunami in Asia that occurred in December 2004. The second leader may be Prime Minister Tony Blair, whose support for George Bush has been unstinting but whose popularity at home has plummeted as a result of involving Great Britain with the USA in the war in Iraq.

[*Century 9, quatrain 4*]

The Asian tsunami

La nef estrange par le tourment marin,
Abordera pres de port incogneu,
Nonobstant signes du rameau palmerin,
Apres mort, pille, bon avis tard venu.

The strange ship because of the storm at sea will approach near an unknown port. Notwithstanding the signs of the palm branches, afterwards death and plunder; good advice comes too late.

This quatrain seems to fit very well with the disaster that hit so much of Asia on 26 December 2004 when a tsunami struck causing widespread death and devastation. Many foreign ships arrived carrying aid, although many of the ports in the region were devastated almost beyond recognition. The advice that came too late could be said to apply to the 'early-warning systems' that exist for earthquakes and tsunamis, which many experts say could have saved many lives, had they been in place.

[*Century 1, quatrain 30*]

Paix ubertré long temps Dieu loüera,
Par tout son regne desert la fleur de lis,
Corps morts d'eau, terre là l'on apporter,
Sperant vain heur d'estre là ensevelis.

Peace and abundance for a long time shall be praised; throughout the period of the reign the fleur-de-lys deserted. Bodies shall be drowned in water, brought there to land, waiting in vain for the hour in which they can be buried.

Nostradamus predicts a devastating flood, the effects of which are so overwhelming that the bodies of those who have been drowned cannot be buried in an organised way. The only disaster that fits the bill is the Asian tsunami in December 2004 and yet the other lines indicate that perhaps this is not the event that was being foretold here.

[*Century 4, quatrain 20*]

2005

Le faux message par election feinte,
Courir par urben rompuë pache arreste,
Voix aceptées, de sang chapelle tainte,
Et à un autre l'empire contraincte.

The false message concerning an election that was rigged will run through the city, arresting the broken pact; voices bought, chapel tainted with blood, to another one, the empire contracted.

There have been many rigged elections and 'voices bought' (people bribed) throughout the course of human history in different parts of the world. It may be that this quatrain applies to the recent election and general situation in Robert Mugabe's Zimbabwe.

[*Century 8, quatrain 20*]

Election of Pope Benedict XVI

Par le trespas du tres vieillard pontife,
Sera esleu Romain de bon aage;
Qu'il sera dit que le Siege debiffe
Et long tiendra & de picquant ouvrage.

By the death of the very aged Pope shall be elected a Roman of good age. It will be said of him that he lessens the position of the Seat, but he will hold it for a long time and with sharp effect.

The death in very old age of the much loved Pope John Paul II in 2005, led to the election of his close friend and colleague, Joseph Ratzinger, Pope Benedict XVI. Many Roman Catholics have expressed disappointment at the election of someone with traditional ideas. But others have said that the new Pope is very much his own man and that the world may well be surprised at the ideas which stem from his papacy.

[*Century 5, quatrain 56*]

2005 onwards

Post-war Iraq

Paix, union sera & changement,
Estats, offices, bas hault, & hault bien bas;
Dresser voyage, le fruict premier, torment,
Guerre cesser, civils proces, debats.

Peace, there will be union and change, estates, offices that were high bought low and those low, high. To prepare for a journey, the first fruits tormented; war ceases, civil processes and debates.

It is tempting to apply this quatrain to post-war Iraq although at the time of writing, the insurgents within that country continue to wreak havoc. But it is the case that those once in high office have been brought low and a successful election has taken place. The various peoples of Iraq are seeking ways to move forwards in union and to form a government that will be respected by all. It is to be hoped that there will indeed be an end to violence and more in the way of debate and civil and legal processes.

[*Century 9, quatrain 66*]

The future of Islam and Russia

La loy Moricque on verra deffaillir,
Apres une autre beaucoup plus seductive,
Boristhenes premier viendra faillir,
Par dons & langues une plus attractive.

The Moorish law will be seen to come to failure, after which another more seductive will arise. Dneiper will be the first to fail by gifts and tongues to another one more attractive.

In this quatrain, Nostradamus seems to link the eventual decline of Islamic influence with the future of Russia. Russia has, of course, undergone enormous changes in recent years and its people appear to find the materialism of the West more attractive that the austerity of communism. However, there is no evidence to date that the influence of Islam is on the decline.

[*Century 3, quatrain 95*]

The eventual defeat of an Islamic nation?

Sur le combat des grands chevaux legers,
On criera le grand croissant confond,
De nuict tuer mont, habits de bergers,
Abismes rouges dans le fossé profond.

At the combat involving the great, light horses, they shall cry out that the great crescent is confounded. To kill by night in the mountains, dressed in the garb of shepherds, red gashes in the deep ditch.

This would appear to describe a historical battle involving cavalry and the defeat of an Eastern force and also, a stealthy attack by men disguised as shepherds, causing a deep ditch to flow red with blood. However, some commentators think that this is a battle between East and West that has yet to take place.

[*Century 7, quatrain 7*]

Forecasts of war, disaster and famine

A pres combat & bataille navale,
Le grand Neptun à son plus haut beffroy,
Rouge adversaire de peur deviendra pasle,
Mettant le grand Ocean en effroy.

After the combat and naval battle, the grand Neptune in his highest steeple; the red adversary shall turn pale in fear, putting the grand ocean in a state of fright.

A great naval battle is forecast here and 'the red adversary' would seem to indicate that a communist power is involved and that it is fearful of the outcome. Great naval battles were fought during the Second World War but it is possible that the one foretold here is yet to come.

[*Century 3, quatrain 1*]

Sera laissé le feu mort vif caché,
Dedans les globes horribles espouventable,
De nuict à classé cité en poudre laché,
La cité à feu, l'ennemy favorable.

Living fire shall be set loose and death hidden, within the globes horrible and fearful, by night the fleet shall pound the city to rubble, the city shall be on fire and this will favour the enemy.

Most commentators believe that this refers to modern warfare due to the reference to fire within globes. It could possibly describe a naval battle during the Second World War but it seems more likely that this is a situation that has thankfully not yet come to pass.

[*Century 5, quatrain 8*]

Vous verrez tost & tard faire grand change,
Horreurs extresmes & vindications,
Que si la lune conduite par son ange,
Le ciel s'approche des inclinations.

You will see great changes made, sooner or later, extreme horrors and vengeances. For as the moon is conducted by its angel, the heavens draw near their inclinations.

This is one of several quatrains depicting disaster connected with particular astrological portents and configurations. Many commentators think that these quatrains most suitably apply to the modern age, perhaps to signs of 'the end of the world' as predicted in the Bible.

[*Century 1, quatrain 56*]

Seront ouys au ciel les armes battre,
Celuy an mesme les divins ennemis,
Voudront loix sainctes injustement debatre,
Par foudre & guerre bien croyants à mort mis.

Then shall be heard in the skies the noise of weapons and battles, in the same year the divine ones are enemies. They shall unjustly debate the holy laws, through storms and war many true believers shall be brought to death.

This quatrain predicts warfare between followers of two different religions and the death of many people as a result. The war is in a modern era due to the reference to aerial fighting.

[*Century 4, quatrain 43*]

L'aisné vaillant de la fille du Roy,
Repoussera si avant les Celtiques,
Qu'il mettra foudres, combien en tel arroy,
Peu & loing puis profondes Hesperiques.

The valiant eldest son of the daughter of the king, shall beat the Celts back very far. He will employ thunderbolts, very many in such an array, little and far, deep into Western lands.

A brave royal leader will attack Western countries and drive their forces back. A modern war is envisaged here using highly effective missiles. Fortunately, this has not yet come to pass.

[*Century 4, quatrain 99*]

La grand famine que je sens approcher,
Souvent tourner puis estre universelle,
Si grande & longue qu'on viendra arracher,
Du bois racine, & l'enfant de mamelle.

The great famine which I sense is approaching will turn from one place to another and then become universal. It will be so great and last for so long that they will pluck roots from the wood and babies from the breast.

This awful depiction of a terrible, widespread famine has already been witnessed on a lesser scale in recent years, particularly in parts of Africa where at times, people have indeed been left with nothing to eat but dried grass and roots. Our television screens have been filled with harrowing pictures of skeletal infants and gaunt, breast-feeding mothers with no milk left for their babies. But here, Nostradamus appears to forecast a famine on an apocalyptic scale, encompassing all regions of the world. At the present time, many experts are forecasting worldwide food shortages as a result of global warming. Some say that as a result of climate change, many productive, crop-growing areas will be lost, either due to the encroachment of deserts, rising sea levels and flooding or due to the fact that the weather will simply become too hot or too cold to sustain plant growth.

[*Century 1, quatrain 67*]

Un peu de temps les temples de couleurs,
De blanc & noir les deux entremeslee;
Rouges & jaunes leur embleront les leurs,
Sang, terre, peste, faim, feu, d'eau affolce.

In a short time, the temples of colours of white and black shall be intermixed. Red and yellow shall take away their emblems, blood, earth, plague, famine, fire, by (want of) water afflicted.

A quatrain that seems to suggest complete racial intermixing—something that is starting to happen with the modern migrations of the peoples of the world. It is to be followed by the familiar catalogue of disasters, according to Nostradamus!

[*Century 6, quatrain 10*]

La voix ouye de l'insolit oyseau,
Sur le canon du respiral estage;
Si haut viendra de froment le boisseau,
Que l'homme d'homme sera Antropophage.

The voice of the unwanted bird having been heard on the high chimney stack; bushels of wheat will rise to a great height and man will resort to man-eating.

A warning of famine brought by an ill-omened bird. The price of wheat will soar through the roof, presumably because of crop failures and become unaffordable and people in the affected area will resort to cannibalism.

[*Century 2, quatrain 75*]

Dans les cyclades en Corinthe & Larisse,
Dedans Sparte tout le Pelloponesse;
Si grand famine, peste, par faux connisse,
Neuf mois tiendra & tout le cherrouesse.

In the Cyclades, in Corinth and Larissa, in Sparta and all the Peloponnesus, there shall be a very great famine, plague caused by a false dust. Nine months will it endure throughout the whole peninsula.

Throughout Greece and the Balkans, famine and disease lasting for nine months is forecast. The reference to 'false dust' strongly suggests a deliberate attack with a biological agent that spreads widely and causes great suffering.

[*Century 5, quatrain 90*]

Si grand famine par une pestifere,
Par pluye longue le long du pole arctique;
Samarobryn cent lieux de l'hemispere,
Vivront sans loy, exempt de politique.

So great a famine and a wave of pestilence, extending its long rain down the length of the Arctic pole; Samorobrin one hundred leagues from the hemisphere, they will live without law and exempt from politics.

A quatrain that has been much discussed and which may indicate famine and plague caused by radioactive fallout or biological attack, extending right over the northern hemisphere of the earth. It may be unleashed from space and the Samorobrin could be a satellite of some kind but law and order will break down, there will be anarchy and everyone who survives will be forced to exist as best they may. A very frightening prospect.

[*Century 6, quatrain 5*]

De la sixiesme claire splendeur celeste,
Viendra tonner si fort eu la Bourgongne;
Puis naistra monstre de tres-hydeuse beste,
Mars, Avril, May, Juin grand charpin & rongne.

From the splendour of the sixth, bright celestial light shall come a very strong thunder to Burgundy. Afterwards shall be born a monster of a very hideous beast; in March, April, May and June, great wounds and worrying.

Saturn is the sixth planet from the sun and in the named months, Nostradamus predicts the birth of a dreadful monster (war?) and carnage and destruction.

[*Century 1, quatrain 80*]

Mars & le sceptre se trouvera conjoint,
Dessous Cancer calamiteuse guerre;
Un peu apres sera nouveau Roy oingt,
Qui par long temps pacifiera la terre.

Mars and the sceptre being conjoined together, under Cancer a calamitous war shall take place. A short while afterwards a new king shall be anointed and for a long time he will give peace to the earth.

While the planet Mars is in conjunction with the Sceptre (Jupiter?), a dreadful war will occur followed by the anointing of a new king whose reign will be one of peace.

[*Century 6, quatrain 24*]

Pour la chaleur solaire sus la mer,
De Negrepont les poissons demy cuits,
Les habitans les viendront entamer,
Quand Rod & Gennes leur faudra le biscuit.

Due to heat like that of the sun upon the sea, at Negrepont the fish will be half baked. The inhabitants will come to cut them up when Rhodes and Genoa shall be in want of food.

Some interpreters of Nostradamus believe that this quatrain predicts severe volcanic eruptions in the Mediterranean region and consequent food shortages. However, others believe that the heating of the sea is a reference to a possible nuclear disaster—either an accident or a bomb, with famine in Greece and Italy in its aftermath.

[*Century 2, quatrain 3*]

Neuf ans le regne le maigre en paix tiendra,
Puis il cherra en soif si sanguinaire,
Pour luy grand peuple sans foy & loy mourra,
Tué par un beaucoup plus debonnaire.

Nine years shall the lean ruler keep his kingdom in peace, then he will fall into a thirst so bloody that a great people will die without faith or law; killed by one very much better than himself.

Some commentators believe that this quatrain has already been fulfilled although it is difficult to connect it to any historical event since Nostradamus' own time. If it has yet to come to pass then it would seem to indicate a grim future for the thin leader and the nation involved.

[*Century 2, quatrain 9*]

> *Trop le ciel pleure l'androgin procreé,*
> *Pres de ciel sang humain respandu,*
> *Par mort trop tarde grand peuple recreé,*
> *Tard & tost vient le secours attendu.*

Too greatly do the heavens weep the birth of the Androgyn, near the skies, human blood shall be spent. Due to the death it is too late for the great nation to be rekindled, late and soon comes the awaited help.

An intriguing quatrain forecasting the birth of a sexless or hermaphrodite leader connected with aerial warfare and the downfall of a great nation for whom help arrives too late. Once again, gloomy predictions of war are made by Nostradamus.

[*Century 2, quatrain 45*]

> *Apres grand trouble humain plus grand s'appreste,*
> *Le grand moteur les siecles renouvelle,*
> *Pluye, sang, laict, famine, feu & peste;*
> *Au ciel feu, courant longue estincelle.*

After a period of great misery for humanity, an even greater one approaches when the great motor of the centuries is renewed. Rain, blood, milk, famine, iron sword and pestilence, and in the sky a fire trailing long sparks.

A quatrain depicting warfare and widespread human misery and then the appearance of a comet around the turn of a century. Many commentators thought that this predicted a third world war at the close of the twentieth century but evidently if this was so, it did not come to pass.

[*Century 2, quatrain 46*]

Mabus puis tost alors mourra viendra,
De gens & bestes une horrible deffaite,
Puis tout à coup la vengeance on verra,
Cent, main, soif, faim, quand courra la comette.

Mabus shall come and then soon die, of men and beasts there will be a horrible destruction. Then all of a sudden the vengeance will be seen, blood, hand, thirst, famine when the comet shall run its course.

Mabus may refer to an Antichrist figure who shall appear, connected with death and destruction. Many have interpreted this as referring to nuclear warfare. All these terrible events will once again happen at the time of the passing of a comet—possible Halley's comet in 2062?

[*Century 2, quatrain 62*]

Le dard du Ciel fera son estenduë,
Morts en parlant grande execution,
La pierre en l'arbre la fiere gent renduë,
Bruit humain monstre, purge expiation.

The dart from heaven shall make its course, some die in the act of speaking, a great execution. The stone in the tree, a fierce people brought low; noise of a human monster, purge and expiation.

This would seem to imply widespread death in a nation caused by a missile attack—launched by a 'human monster', supposedly to purge and expiate former wrongs.

[*Century 2, quatrain 70*]

Quand le deffaut du soleil lors sera,
Sur le plein jour le monstre sera veu;
Tout autrement on l'interpretera,
Cherté n'a garde, nul n'y aura pourveu.

2005 onwards

When the eclipse of the sun shall be present, in plain daylight will the monster be seen. It will be interpreted in other ways, they will care nothing about the dearth for none have made preparations for it.

The monster that appears around the time of an eclipse of the sun may be a metaphor for a famine for which people are ill-prepared or it could be meant to be interpreted literally. A total solar eclipse that was visible in the south-west of England, much of Europe, the Middle East and Asia occurred in August 1999, as the turn of the century approached—always a portentous period for Nostradamus. An annular solar eclipse occurred in 2003 and other eclipses will take place during the course of the twenty-first century. Sadly, famine for which we are ill-prepared is all too common in Africa and was present in 1999, 2003 and 2005 but Nostradamus may have been forecasting food shortages closer to home, perhaps as a result of climate change.

[*Century 3, quatrain 34*]

L'enfant naistra à deux dents en la gorge,
Pierre en Tulcie par pluye tomberont;
Peu d'ans apres ne sera bled ne orge,
Pour faouller ceux qui de faim failliront.

A child shall be born with two teeth in his mouth, stones will fall on the ground in Tuscany like rain. A few years afterwards there shall be neither wheat nor barley to satisfy those who become weak with hunger.

A child who presumably is destined to be a person of some importance is born with two, fully formed teeth and there are showers of stones in Tuscany. This could refer to a rare natural event or possibly something man-made. Then Nostradamus makes yet another prediction about crop failures and famine.

[*Century 3, quatrain 42*]

Global warming: a great flood

Par la tumeur de Heb., Po, Tag., Tybre de Rome,
Et par l'estang Geman & Aretin,
Les deux grands chefs & citez de Garonne,
Prins, morts, noyez, partir humain butin.

Due to the swelling of the Ebro, Po, Tagus, Tiber of Rome and the Lake Geneva and those of Arezzo, the two great, chief cities of Garonne are taken, dead, drowned. The human booty divided.

A great flood with consequent devastation and death by drowning is forecast here, covering a huge part of Europe. One can only hope that this quatrain will prove to be inaccurate.

[*Century 3, quatrain 12*]

An astrological quatrain

La grand estoille par sept jours bruslera,
Nuë fera deux soleils apparoir,
Le gros mastin toute nuict hurlera,
Quand grand pontife changera de terroir.

The great star shall burn for seven days and the cloud will make two suns appear. The huge mastiff will howl throughout the night when the great pontiff shall change his territory.

The first lines appear to refer to a comet and many commentators previously thought that the events foretold here referred to the 1986 appearance of Halley's comet or perhaps to comet Hale-Bopp, first seen in our skies in 1997. The time reference seems to be more appropriate to comet Hale-Bopp as it passed closest to the earth on 23 March 1997 and then, seven days later, made its nearest approach to the sun. Comets are, in fact, enormous blocks of ice that burn (boil) away as they approach the sun, forming a trail—the comet's 'tail'. However, the Pope did not change his place of residence during the time of the appearance of either of these comets so perhaps these events will come to pass in 2062, when Halley's comet is due to make its next visit.

[*Century 2, quatrain 41*]

> *Le monde proche du dernier periode,*
> *Saturne encor tard sera de retour;*
> *Translat empier devers nation Brodde;*
> *L'œil arraché à Narbon par autour.*

The world approaches its final period, Saturn is again late in his return. The empire shall be changed towards the black nation, an eye shall be plucked out at Narbonne by a hawk.

An astrological quatrain foretelling the rise to prominence of an African country, but not without strife, as indicated by the reference to Saturn. This shall take place during the run-up to the 'final period' or the end of the world, according to Nostradamus.

[*Century 3, quatrain 92*]

Religious beliefs

> *Le corps sans ame plus n'estre en sacrifice,*
> *Jour de mort mis en nativité,*
> *L'esprit divin fera l'ame felice*
> *Voyant le verbe en son eternité.*

The body without a soul no longer brought to the sacrifice. At the day of death brought to rebirth. The divine spirit shall make the soul joyful by seeing the word in its eternity.

This seems to be a statement of Nostradamus' personal beliefs, possibly revealed to him during his mystical studies about what happens to a person after death. It has very evident Christian overtones but the meaning of the first line is obscure.

[*Century 2, quatrain 13*]

The third Antichrist

Un jour seront amis les deux grands maistres,
Leur grand pouvoir se verra augmenté;
La terre neufue sera en ses hauts estres,
Au sanguinaire, le nombre racompté.

One day the two great masters will be friends, their great power shall be seen to increase. The new land shall be at the pinnacle of its influence, to the man of blood the number will be recounted.

Two great world leaders will become friends and allies and by the reference to the 'new land', one of these is certainly the leader of America. It seems likely that the other power may be China and certainly, relations between these two great nations have improved of late. Nostradamus warns here that the 'man of blood', a sinister and evil figure who is also referred to in other quatrains, is watching from the wings and keeping a close eye on developments, presumably preparing to strike when he deems that the time is ripe.

[*Century 2, quatrain 89*]

Sa main derniere par Alus sanguinaire,
Ne se pourra plus la mer garentir;
Entre deux fleuves craindre main militaire,
Le noir l'ireux le fera repentir.

His last hand by the bloody Alus, he shall be unable to guarantee his safety by sea. Between two rivers shall he fear the military hand, the black and angry one will cause him to repent.

The identity of Alus is not known but it could be yet another reference to the third Antichrist figure who will go to war with an African nation.

[*Century 6, quatrain 33*]

> *Contre les rouges sectes se banderont,*
> *Feu, eau, fer, corde par paix se minera,*
> *Au point mourir ceux qui machineront,*
> *Fors un que monde sur tout ruynera.*

Against the reds sects will be ranged, fire, water, iron, the rope will ruin by peace. At the point of death are those who hatch plots, except the one who above all others shall bring ruin to the world.

This quatrain seems to forecast war against a communist nation brought about by various people. It certainly could be related to the breaking away of former communist states, such as Georgia, from Russian influence. However, the last line appears to again forecast the eventual coming of another fearful Antichrist figure who will bring ruination to the world.

[*Century 9, quatrain 51*]

A revelation will be made in 2055

> *De cinq cens ans plus compte l'on tiendra,*
> *Celuy qu'estoit l'ornement de son temps,*
> *Puis à un coup grande clarté donrra,*
> *Que par ce siecle les rendra tres contens.*

For a further 500 years they will take account of him who was the ornament of his own time. Then all of a sudden a great light shall be shed which will make the people of that century very contented.

In this quatrain, Nostradamus is speaking of himself and predicting that 500 years after his own death, a startling revelation will be made which will be widely known and believed by the people of that time. If this is so, we can look for this revelation around the year 2055.

[*Century 3, quatrain 94*]

Miscellaneous

D'habits nouveaux apres fait la treuve,
Malice, tramme & machination;
Premier mourra qui en sera la preuve,
Couleur Venise insidiation.

After a truce is achieved, new clothes are put on, malice, plotting and machination. He who shall prove it shall be the first to die, under the colour of the treachery of Venice.

This strange quatrain seems to predict treachery, political assassination and manoeuvring in Venice which, in earlier times, was a city state but is now a part of Italy.

[*Century 4, quatrain 6*]

Par detracteur calomnié à puis nay;
Quand istront faicts enormes & martiaux;
La moindre part dubieuse a l'aisné,
Et tost au regne seront faicts partiaux.

There shall be calumny uttered by a detractor against the younger born, when enormous and martial deeds are carried out. The least part doubtful to the eldest one and soon in the realm there shall be partisan actions.

This quatrain could be said to have overtones relating to Blair, Bush and the Iraq war but it is also quite general and may not have happened yet. Prime Minister Tony Blair has certainly had to endure the allegations of many detractors who have accused him of falsehood in taking Great Britain into a war of disputed legality. President George Bush, on the other hand, has apparently suffered few doubts and his personal position does not appear to have been greatly harmed by the war. Iraq, in the meantime, continues to suffer the horrors of insurgent attacks on a daily basis but many would call this terrorism rather than 'partisan actions'.

[*Century 6, quatrain 95*]

Death of a king

Quand on viendra le grand Roy parenter,
Avant qu'il ait du tout l'ame renduë;
Celuy qui moins le viendra lamenter,
Par Lyons, d'Aigles, Croix, Couronne venduë.

When they will come to administer to the great king the last rites, before he has quite given up his soul, he who will come last to lament him, by lions, eagles, crosses, crowns sold.

A quatrain depicting the death of a great king whom many come to mourn, bearing with them their heraldic arms. One important personage seems to be particularly affected by the death. This may have taken place already or possibly describes a future king whose passing attracts pomp and ceremony. If it were not for the fact that a king is referred to quite clearly, it would be tempting to say that this could apply to the death of Pope John Paul II in 2005.

[*Century 6, quatrain 71*]

Aux temples saints seront faits grands scandales,
Comptez seront par honneur & loüanges,
D'un que l'on gravé d'argent, d'or les medalles,
La fin sera en tourmens bien estranges.

In the sacred temples scandals shall be made, they shall be considered as honours and worthy of praise. By one whom they engrave on silver and gold medals, the end shall be in torments that are very strange.

Although it is likely that some kind of religious scandal is being referred to here, it is also possible to attribute this quatrain to drug cheating among certain (Olympic) athletes who have received honours, praise and medals at the time, only to later be stripped of them when the scandal breaks.

[*Century 6, quatrain 9*]

The supernatural

Les os des pieds & des mains enserrez,
Par bruit maison long temps inhabitée,
Seront par songes concavant deterrez,
Maison salubre & sans bruit habitee.

The bones of the feet and the hands in manacles, because of the noise (of the ghost) the house is uninhabited for a very long time. Then by a dream of digging the bones shall be unearthed, the house restored to health and inhabited without any further noise.

This is a very interesting quatrain, graphically describing the haunting of a house by an unquiet spirit whose earthly remains are shackled somewhere in the walls or floor, the inference being that the person was murdered or left to die. Someone connected with the house has a dream that reveals the location of the skeleton and presumably it is removed and given a proper burial. The haunting and noise in the house ceases and people are able to live there in peace once again.

Borley Rectory in Essex was said to be haunted by the ghost of a nun. One of the many stories concerning her was that she was a French woman who had run away to Borley with her lover. Soon afterwards, during a violent argument, the lover killed her but whether by accident or design is not known. He was said to have buried the body in the cellar of the old house and many years later, a female skull and jawbone were discovered, along with some religious artefacts. However, in the case of Borley, the noises and sightings of the ghost did not cease with the discovery of the remains and continued even after the old house was burned down in 1939.

Stories such as this are common throughout history and among all peoples and cultures and we will probably never know the details of the particular haunting that Nostradamus foresaw in this quatrain.

[*Century 7, quatrain 41*]